P9-CFN-081

Learning
from
the Heart

LESSONS ON LIVING, LOVING, AND LISTENING

DANIEL GOTTLIEB

STERLING

New York / London
www.sterlingpublishing.com

Author's proceeds from the sale of this book are being donated to children's charities. The author and publisher are grateful for permission to quote from the following:

"Fearing Paris," by Marsha Truman Cooper, originally published by *River City* published in the re-issued chapbook, *Substantial Holdings*, by Pudding House, 2002;

"Mother Knows Best" from *Wounded Healers* (page 35) by Rachel Naomi Remen, M.D., published by Wounded Healer Press copyright ©1994 by Rachel Naomi Remen, by kind permission of the author;

Lines from *The Prophet* by Kahlil Gibran, copyright ©1923 by Kahlil Gibran and renewed 1951 by Administrators C.T.A. of Kahlil Gibran Estate and Mary G. Gibran, used by permission of Alfred A. Knopf, a division of Random House, Inc.;

"Love after Love" from *Collected Poems 1948-1984* by Derek Walcott, copyright © 1986 by Derek Walcott, reprinted by permission of Farrar, Straus and Giroux, LLC.

Library of Congress Cataloging-in-Publication Data

Gottlieb, Daniel, 1946-
  Learning from the heart : lessons on living, loving, and listening / Daniel Gottlieb.
    p. cm.
  ISBN-13: 978-1-4027-4999-5
  ISBN-10: 1-4027-4999-6
  1. Conduct of life. I. Title.
  BJ1521.G635 2008
  170'.44--dc22

                                    2007035100

10 9 8 7 6 5 4 3 2 1

Published by Sterling Publishing Co., Inc.
387 Park Avenue South, New York, NY 10016
Copyright © 2008 by Daniel Gottlieb
Distributed in Canada by Sterling Publishing
c/o Canadian Manda Group, 165 Dufferin Street
Toronto, Ontario, Canada M6K 3H6
Distributed in the United Kingdom by GMC Distribution Services
Castle Place, 166 High Street, Lewes, East Sussex, England BN7 1XU
Distributed in Australia by Capricorn Link (Australia) Pty. Ltd.
P.O. Box 704, Windsor, NSW 2756, Australia

Manufactured in the United States of America
All rights reserved

Sterling ISBN-13: 978-1-4027-4999-5
          ISBN-10: 1-4027-4999-6

For information about custom editions, special sales, premium and corporate purchases, please contact Sterling Special Sales Department at 800-805-5489 or specialsales@sterlingpublishing.com.

Dedication

I dedicate this book to my precious daughters, Alison and Debra.

Your births opened my heart to a lifetime of love and devotion.

I have watched you crawl and walk and fall in love and rebel. I've watched you get hurt and suffer—and then heal. With delight and awe I have watched your bodies, your minds, and your souls develop.

Now I watch you love whom you love with grace and compassion, devoting yourselves to making the world more just for those who need justice.

We have brought each other great love and blessings. In the past, your lives were in my hands and that brought me joy. In the future, my life will be in your hands and that brings me peace.

May we awaken from the illusion that we are different.
—Thich Nhat Hanh

CONTENTS

Introduction

❧

December 20, 1979, was a clear, crisp day that started like any other. I was a thirty-three-year-old psychologist doing quite well in my profession as director of an outpatient substance abuse program. I was blessed to have a beautiful wife and two young daughters who were just beginning their school day. At seven thirty in the morning I kissed my family goodbye and walked across the frozen lawn to climb into my Dodge Dart. Today, I can still hear the crackle of the lawn under my feet. I remember that sound because those were the last steps I would ever take. One hour later, while driving on the Pennsylvania Turnpike, I looked up in the sky to see a big black object coming toward my windshield. The next thing I remembered was waking up at Ephrata Hospital and learning that I was a quadriplegic.

Sure, I experienced all of the emotions people feel after a trauma: shock, grief, rage, and of course terror. But in hindsight, what was most painful and most terrifying was feeling disconnected from my fellow humans. Over the next several weeks, I began to wonder about what it really meant to be human. Can I truly be human if I can't stand up for my beliefs? I asked myself. How about if I can't make love like normal men, or even dance with my wife?

Am I human if I can't live without nurses and medications, if I must spend my life in wheelchairs?

To cope with this terrible sense of alienation, I began to simply notice what humans (they and I) did—how we acted and reacted, how feelings worked and how thoughts and emotions played off one another. I just noticed without judgment or analysis. I needed to do this to understand what it really meant to be human and to reassure myself that I was still one of them. And yet, deep down, I knew that although I might be one of them, from this point on, I was different.

❧

As I lay in my hospital bed, I began to observe that most people, even my doctors, seemed uncomfortable when they were around me. I could tell by the way they raised their voices just a little bit when they spoke with me, or didn't make eye contact, or spoke quickly. I could tell they were anxious when they tried to make me feel or think differently about what it meant to be a quadriplegic.

So I noticed that humans get anxious when they face something or someone that is unusual. They do lots of different things to manage their discomfort and anxiety. Some tried to make me happier. Others tried to convince me (and themselves) that it wasn't really as bad as I thought it was. And some people (like my closest friend) I never saw again. But they were all doing the same thing: feeling anxious and trying not to. That's what we humans do.

When I was with these anxious people, everyone's hearts were closed because of their anxiety. Anxiety tends to close our hearts, our minds, and even our eyes. That seemed quite human to me, because people with anxiety do suffer, and we all want to diminish suffering however we can. And when I looked inside, I noticed that anxiety is contagious. When I was with anxious people, I felt closed off. I found myself either arguing with what they were saying, or just nodding and not really listening. But even when I wasn't listening, I was feeling. And when people tried to make me "feel better," I usually felt lonely, misunderstood, and frightened.

Sitting in the occupational therapy department about six weeks after my accident, I remember feeling great despair as I looked up at the drab olive cinderblock wall. I said to no one in particular, "Who would have thought I would come to a place like this to die?"

My occupational therapist was sitting right next to me and quickly said, "No, Dan, you didn't come here to die; you came here to live." Of course, on one level she was right. But so was I. I knew I had to deal with death before I could face life. And because she made that statement, I felt more isolated and misunderstood.

I also saw that there were some people who *didn't* feel anxious around me. I never figured out why, because I wasn't really in the business of figuring things out. I was in the business of observing. And when I was with people who were not anxious, I noticed they were asking about me and listening. And they were telling me about themselves.

I felt that their only goal was to be with me. They didn't need to change anything. When I was with these people, I felt safe and relaxed. I felt less alone.

Finally, there was a third category of people who did feel anxious around me but *knew* they were anxious and talked to me about it. They were able, somehow, to be comfortable with themselves even when they were anxious. I felt safe with these people also. But there was an extra dimension here: When people told me about the anxiety and suffering they experienced as a result of my accident, I felt great love and compassion for them. Several times, I held people in my arms as they wept about what happened to me.

In the face of unexpected tragedy, humans have lots of different reactions. And those reactions get dealt with in many ways. When humans around me were anxious, I was anxious. When they were open and nurturing, I felt safe. And when they felt vulnerable, I was nurturing, and we both felt better.

In those first few days, I was beginning to learn that emotions are contagious. Even unfelt emotions.

WHAT I'VE LEARNED ABOUT LOVE

*Love cures people—both the ones
who give and the ones who receive it.*
—Dr. Karl Menninger

In the movie *Divine Secrets of the Ya-Ya Sisterhood,* the father, played by James Garner, is walking along with his daughter, played by Sandra Bullock, when she confronts him with the question, "Daddy, were you loved enough in your life?"

Her words express the unmet wishes of that child. In the movie, her mother is portrayed as a character who is overly emotional and self-absorbed. Though the mother gets married and has a child, she is clearly not able to love her daughter properly. And the young girl carries the burden. The daughter is angry and resentful—resulting from deprivation of love—which is what makes her question so poignant.

As for the father, in the movie it is apparent he wasn't loved nearly enough. Yet . . . there he is, walking along side by side with the daughter he loves dearly, and it's clear that he's happy. It's a Hollywood cliché. But it occurred to me that his daughter was asking the wrong question. It isn't whether he was loved enough. The question should be, "Daddy, did you *love* enough?"

I think the Beatles got it wrong when they said, "Love is all you need." But Andrew Lloyd Webber got it right when he said, "Love changes everything." Whether it's love given and received or love promised and betrayed—whichever way you examine it—love changes everything. And no love is more profound than pure, openhearted selfless love.

The best example of this love is when we see our child for the first time. Our heart is fully open, and it feels as if all the love we have ever felt or could feel is happening to us right now. Almost all parents, at that moment, make a solemn promise to love and protect the child from harm forever.

It is that promise that gets us in trouble. Because of our natural desire to protect our children, we develop anxiety. We are more vigilant about potential dangers in our children's surroundings and sometimes worry about their every move. That's adaptive. Children wouldn't survive without it. We worry because we adore our children. But when we are worrying, we cannot feel our adoration. And so it goes—as our children get bigger, the anxiety gets bigger, while our ability to feel that great, openhearted love gets smaller. It's still in there, but we can't access it as easily.

Love rarely remains pure and selfless. Sometimes when we think of those we love, we worry whether they love us back as much or if they are happy. We may believe that our anxiety is a way of "looking after them" or that it's "in their best interest." But when we try to make them feel differently or get them to change "for their own good," that's not love. That's anxiety. It's the kind of anxiety that makes us want to change things so that we can feel better. I have watched many people try to change their partners in intimate relationships so that they can recapture that initial feeling of adoration or security.

I'm sure there are as many descriptions of love as there are human beings who have tried to describe it. Dr. Stephen Post, president of the Institute for Research on Unlimited Love at Case Western Reserve University, describes altruistic love as a love for all humanity without exception, with abiding kindness and service. This love is a selfless act of generosity of spirit. And sometimes it's really a state of being. There are times when I have experienced love that doesn't feel like action at all. I'm not feeling love for someone—or for something I do. Instead, there are moments when I feel that my *being* is love.

Of course that feeling of *being love* doesn't last long for any of us. I don't think it can, without several lifetimes of practice. But if we're lucky, there are times when we do experience that feeling.

Early one spring morning not long ago, I got a call from my daughter Ali. She had been having neck pain for several weeks. When she said the pain was severe and radiating down her arm, that scared me. And then she told me she'd already had an MRI and that she had a ruptured disc between the fifth and sixth cervical vertebrae. That nearly put me over the edge. That's because my spinal cord is severed between the fifth and sixth cervical vertebrae. Finally she told me that her neurosurgeon wanted her to have surgery within the next several days.

So I did what I do best. I told Ali about my concerns and asked her permission to get a second opinion. Though she trusted her doctor, she agreed that a second opinion would be a good idea. Full of adrenaline, I contacted all of my doctor friends who, in turn, contacted all of their neurology/neurosurgeon friends. Within two days, I had several other opinions, and all the doctors I consulted agreed with the first opinion. Ali should have surgery right away.

When Ali and I spoke on the telephone about the findings, she said she would call her doctor and have surgery the next morning. In the middle of the conversation, she asked me if she should prepare "some kind of will." I casually replied that it would probably be a good idea. I didn't think much about that statement, because I quickly had to make arrangements to travel early the next morning to a hospital in New York State, so I could be with Ali.

The following morning, I met my daughter at the hospital. Her partner, Geoffrey, was sitting beside her. She looked frightened. And as the time for surgery approached, she began to cry. Geoffrey and I sat with her as long as they allowed us to. I couldn't feel my own emotions because I was busy caring for my child. Two hours later, the doctor came out to give us a wonderful report. He said Ali had done quite well and even reported diminished pain immediately after surgery. Yet I still didn't feel the great relief I had expected; I just felt very sleepy and quiet.

Several hours later, Ali was sitting in a chair in her room, Geoffrey beside her holding her hand. The scene was truly amazing, better than I ever hoped for, and still I didn't feel great relief.

By the next morning, Ali had recovered almost full strength in her arm and she was ready to be discharged. As we sat in the lobby waiting for Geoffrey to get the car, she looked over at me and said, "I was really scared I was going to die in there. Were you?"

I said what I believed to be true: "I really wasn't afraid you were going to die. I wasn't even afraid of quadriplegia. I was afraid your arm would be paralyzed."

A few minutes later, we kissed goodbye. Ali got into Geoffrey's car and I got into my van. We returned to our respective homes.

Over the next several hours, I thought about our final conversation in the lobby and began to feel nauseated and quite agitated. And then I remembered that forty-eight hours earlier Ali and I had talked about her will. *I* hadn't been thinking about losing my daughter, but my body had. Of course I was terrified, but I couldn't feel my feelings. Not only were they too big, but I had things to do. But those feelings were still there.

Throughout the course of the evening the day after Ali's surgery, I became even more agitated. I felt the panic, terror, and helplessness my body had felt forty-eight hours earlier. And I hated it. I wanted to do almost anything to avoid the feelings. All those emotions found their way into my consciousness, and as a consequence the emotional pain was unbearable. My instinct was to do whatever I could to make that pain go back underground. I didn't sleep well that night, and had a difficult couple of days thereafter. I didn't enjoy the pain I experienced. But I'm glad I felt it.

A few weeks later, I invited my friend Kim to come over to the house for Passover Seder. We were joined by Ali and Geoffrey, who drove down from Ali's home in North Jersey with her three-legged dog, Marley. It was the first time I'd seen Ali since her surgery, and I was just thrilled. She was stiff and couldn't move her neck, but she was filled with energy and animation. Geoffrey's parents were there, and so were my daughter, Debbie; her husband, Pat; and my grandson, Sam. At age seven—the age I fell in love with baseball—he was just learning how to play. And he was good at it. So after dinner Sam and Pat, and Geoffrey and his dad all went out in the backyard to play ball while the rest of us watched from the porch. Sam was hitting the ball. Pat, his father, was standing behind him, catching. Geoffrey was pitching, and Geoffrey's father was playing the field.

From the porch, we could hear Pat saying to Sam, "Sam, put on your 'game' face!" Sam put on a serious grimace. And I hollered down from the porch, "Sam, that doesn't look like a game face! That looks like you're taking a poop!"

Everyone laughed. Then the foursome resumed their game while the rest of us up on the porch started talking and . . .

There was a moment I noticed all that. And I knew

how fragile it was. Ali wakes up one day with neck pain, and it all changes. Debbie has back pain. I see a black thing in the sky. Or tomorrow I wake with a fever. . . .

And because I realized the fragility of life, that moment felt perfect. And I was so grateful. I felt love.

It seems as if the more we let go, the more we experience love. Love is beyond everything else—anxiety, desire, hope, resentment. Love is openhearted, demands nothing, and needs nothing. It is more likely to visit when our desires are quiet, when we don't need or want much, and when we accept that everything we love is not permanent but is with us at this very moment.

So Who Do We Think
We Are, Anyway?

∽⋊⋉∾

When Ali's beloved three-legged dog, Marley, comes to any family gathering, she is treated with just as much respect as a human. And in many ways, she seems very human indeed. But I do sense that Marley is oblivious to the fact that she's missing something. Yes, she has three legs instead of four. But to Marley that doesn't seem to matter.

Marley really doesn't mind a missing leg. When Ali takes Marley for a walk, people react in interesting and predictable ways. They tend to feel sorry for her (especially if they're kids). They want to know what happened to her, how she lost her leg. But after people have watched Marley for a few minutes, they realize that the dog doesn't care. And neither does Ali.

Ali says that Marley reminds her of me.

Losing a leg and breaking a neck are what I consider narcissistic injuries. Note, however: Animals and humans react quite differently to such bodily insults. Humans have a "self" image, an image of the way we think our lives should be. If we lose a leg or break a neck, the self-image changes. Animals don't have that sense of "self." When they are injured, it doesn't mean anything to them. Of course they know whether or not they are in pain, and they feel better when they're not. But because they don't have egos, injuries and disabilities are simply facts.

I don't want to sound envious of Marley, but I do think life without a self-image, an ego, is quite different from what we experience as humans. I have been watching dogs and have learned this: They love life fully. We seem to cherish life, but most of us aren't fully aware of this day by day. Dogs seem to know that life is good. Dogs also know about altruistic love. Because they don't have egos, they seem to love loving. When we humans love, most of us are timid about opening our hearts all the way. The ego wonders: "Will I be hurt? Will I be loved back? Will my needs get met or will I be abandoned?" Dogs don't have these questions. They just love.

Death seems like less of a problem to animals, too. They love life but they don't fear death. Death is a problem for us because it is the ultimate narcissistic insult. How could I die? How could the world go on, and everything be just the same, without me here?

Death is rude. But to Marley and her sisters and brothers, losing a life is like losing a leg.

Part of being human is developing an identity. Infants as young as three years old go through a stage where they start to run away from their parents. Typically they'll dash a short distance, then stop and look back to see if they're being chased. That's just the beginning, of course. What they're starting to do is build an identity separate from their parents.

We do that forever. "Who am I?" "Who am I supposed to be?" "Who *should* I be?"

How do we answer those questions in a world that says, "Be all that you can be"? (Or, as I heard on another commercial not long ago, "Good enough is no longer good enough!") How do we find our identity in a world that insists your identity is defined by your achievements, by your beauty, by your power, by your youth?

As people work hard to become who they think they *should* be . . . and work even harder to avoid becoming the person they fear they *could* be, the search for identity goes on . . . and on . . . and on.

Now here's the funny thing about it. Identity is an illusion, anyway. We work so hard for it, but it's an illusion. Having an identity is like having a handful of water: Right when we think we have hold of something, it slips through our fingers.

Who are you at this moment? You are a reader; you're an intellectual and a searcher. At this moment. Who else are you at this moment? Probably someone who is looking for information that will validate your illusion of an identity, of a belief system. And if you find it in this book, then you will probably say it's a good book.

But all those labels can change when you start to do something else, or when your mind moves in a different direction, or when you're in another environment. Everything changes—and that includes you. Yet we have the need to find our identity. We have to see what makes us bleed and discover what makes us heal. We need to seek the boundaries where our power begins and ends. That's all part of running away, looking back, and running away again. (Psychologists call it rapprochement.)

Part of wisdom is learning that the identity can be dispensed with. It's when we realize that that pronoun "I" is written with invisible ink.

People introduce me as a psychologist and a therapist and an author and a parent and a quadriplegic and on and on. But really *who I am* is a being who breathes, who feels fear and longing and love and lust and hatred and revulsion and shame. That's all part of the water passing through my fingers. I feel my irrelevance and then I find fear, and then sadness, and then peace.

Rainer Maria Rilke has a poem that includes the line, "I am much too small in this world, yet not small enough to be to you just object and thing, dark and smart." How do we live if we're not as big as we think we should be, if we don't have deep anchors to hold us in place? Who are we if we give up the labels of "parent" or "good" or "devoted and loving" or "tough and stubborn"? How do we live without an identity that we can lean on?

Marley knows.

Over the years I've worked with many people who have had a variety of illnesses. Some with relatively minor illnesses were devastated while others with catastrophic illnesses seemed to be doing pretty well. One pair of couples—I've written about them before—demonstrate this dynamic well, and the experience of treating them simultaneously taught me a lesson I have never forgotten. Both couples were dealing with quadriplegia. The first couple was in their early twenties and recently married. These were two people in the process of building their identities—starting their careers, thinking about creating their family. The young man had been studying to become a state trooper when he was in a car accident and became a quadriplegic. They were devastated. The man became bitter; his young wife became severely depressed. The relationship broke up.

That same year, I worked with a couple in their sixties who had been married nearly forty years. The husband was driving a construction truck that turned over, and he broke his neck. As it happened, the fracture was in exactly the same place as the younger man's, so their quadriplegia was identical.

My therapy with the older couple took just a few sessions. They wanted to know how to make love. The woman wanted to know if it was okay to leave her husband alone when she went grocery shopping. She talked about feeling guilty when she went out to the movies with her friends. We discussed some of the practical steps they would have to take to deal with his quadriplegia.

And that was all. In just a few sessions, we were done.

To the older couple, the accident was an event in their lives. It didn't change who they were and how much they loved each other. To the younger couple, the husband's quadriplegia shattered their lives. Both couples were dealing with exactly the same event and both faced the same physical challenges, but quadriplegia meant something vastly different to each of them.

We don't say that one couple is strong and the other is weak. We can't even say that one of the couples is more resilient. The difference is in the size and shape of the "I." For the older couple, like most people blessed with wisdom, the "I" is smaller and softer. And the accident is just an event.

BUT I KEEP HOLDING ON

Anne, a woman in her forties, came to see me during a difficult time. She said she felt as if she had spent the first twenty or thirty years of her life trying to climb to the top of a tree.

"Well, I got there," Anne said, "and now I think it's the wrong tree."

I asked her why she was coming into therapy.

"I find myself climbing again," she said. "And *this time*, I want to make sure it's the right tree."

I asked, "Why are you climbing?"

When we talked more about it, we were really talking about her theory: "If I climb . . . and if it's the right tree . . . then I will be happy with my life."

So she was looking for another tree. But her theory didn't change. She really believed that if she could find the right tree or ladder or path, she would find happiness.

My theory is that everyone has theories that they're not aware of: "If I lose weight, I'll be happier with myself." Or: "If my spouse changes, I'll have a happy family life." "If I get the promotion, everything will be fine." "If my child gets into Harvard, he (or she) will have the advantages that I didn't have." "If I hang out with successful people, I'll turn into a success."

And there are negative theories, too: "If I don't get my work done, I'll lose my job" or "If we don't earn more money, we won't be able to pay our bills and . . ."

Invariably, these theories are wrong. I don't mean it's wrong to have them—that's what we all do. What I mean is, they're just theories. Sometimes we create our own theories, but just as often we are handed our theories by our parents or our religion. Sometimes our theories come from trends in the culture. These theories can give our lives structure and help us feel less anxious. But even when their theories don't work, most people don't change them. They simply work even harder on the old ones. And often as not, those theories keep us stuck.

So how do we get unstuck?

Whenever I'm in distress or feel great anxiety about some future event, I picture the worst thing that could possibly happen. And then I try to figure out a way to live with that consequence. Once when my editor at the *Philadelphia Inquirer* harshly criticized one of my columns, I felt terrible anxiety and shame. So I took my fears to the worst-case scenario and imagined either getting fired or resigning from a job that I love. For the next several days, I lived as if I was no longer a columnist. Not surprisingly, the fear diminished pretty quickly.

Before my surgeries, I would ask myself, "What is the outcome I am most afraid of? Inevitably, presurgical fear is about death. So I spent some time imagining what my children's lives would be like without me. When I spend time with my nightmare, rather than running away from it, the anxiety dissipates.

When my grandson Sam was diagnosed with autism, I put myself in a place where he had the most severe symptoms and imagined what life would be like for him, for his parents, and for me. Now when I have patients who say, "I couldn't possibly live without . . . ," I encourage them to finish that sentence. What if your theory is wrong? What if you can live without whatever it is you believe you can't?

John, a middle-aged man I worked with, grew up in a large family with a volatile, alcoholic father. Somehow, as John grew older he came to believe that he was responsible for holding the family together. If he didn't "do his job" as the family's caretaker and peacemaker—so went his theory—everything would fall apart. So that's what he tried to do. He cared for his siblings, for his nieces and nephews, and then he took on the role of caring for his parents as they aged. He held to the theory that he was *the one*. He had to do this . . . or else! And he really organized his life around this theory. It kept him up at night. It exhausted him because he was constantly traveling around the country looking after all the family members who would otherwise "fall apart."

When John came to see me, he was depressed. His marriage and his health were in jeopardy. As we talked about this theory he was barely aware of, he came to recognize how firmly he believed it to be absolutely true.

So I asked him to imagine the worst—his family falling apart. He did. As he played out the consequences, he imagined that one sibling would end up dead, another would be hospitalized, and another would be so ostracized she would never talk to her other siblings. We just sat there for a while trying to examine what his life would look like, day by day, if that happened.

John's nightmare became more bearable. Not pleasant, just more bearable. And that gave him the courage to re-examine his theory. If he could live with the possibility that his family *would* fall apart, could he take a risk and entertain the possibility that they *wouldn't*?

And that's the most difficult part of this theory business. We keep holding on to our theories because it's all we have. To let go of something we've always believed in requires a leap of faith—trust in something that is unknowable. And I think the task for all of us is to have faith in our own resilience. When that happens, we are exposed to many more possibilities.

By the way, during the course of my work with Anne, who was searching for the right tree to climb, she felt she discovered something important. She came to believe that she wasn't really in the pursuit of happiness, that she climbed because she was just a climber—a searcher—and always had been. She realized she was climbing trees because she loved to explore and learn. When she let go of her old theory—that she'd find happiness at the top of the right tree—she no longer judged herself as a success or failure. When the judgment stopped, her life turned into something to be experienced rather than managed.

Fearing Paris

Marsha Truman Cooper

Suppose that what you fear
could be trapped
and held in Paris.
Then you would have
the courage to go
everywhere in the world.
All the directions of the compass
open to you,
except the degrees east or west
of true north
that lead to Paris.
Still, you wouldn't dare
put your toes smack dab on the city limit line.
You're not really willing to stand on a mountainside
miles away,
and watch the Paris lights
come up at night.
Just to be on the safe side,
you decide to stay completely out of France.
But then danger
seems too close
even to those boundaries,
and you feel the timid part of you
covering the whole globe again.
You need the kind of friend
who learns your secret and says,
"See Paris first."

Living Under the Bell Curve

I'm going to tell a story that I've told before, of a true revelation in my life. The lesson began in third grade, but it was not until I was well into my adult years that I understood what it meant.

In third grade, my teacher, Mrs. McNesbit, created a merit-recognition system that was reflected by the seating arrangements. If we got our reading lessons right on a given day, we'd move our chairs up toward the front of the classroom. If we didn't do well, we'd move down the row, toward the back of the classroom. So chairs were moved every day all over the place.

Over the course of the year, I was not consistent. For a brief time, I was in the last seat in the back row, and for an even briefer moment I occupied the first seat in the first row. But by the end of the year I was the last seat in the second row—somewhere around the sixtieth percentile. At the end of the year I remember thinking, "If only I had another week, I could work harder and get to the front row. If not the first seat, I could be close to that."

That image stayed in my brain for twenty years. Then I was a young professional, doing extremely well, helping many people, getting the respect of my colleagues and supervisors, yet still pushing myself, still believing that I wasn't quite where I could be and that if I only worked harder and accomplished more, I could get to where I thought I belonged. I was twenty-eight years old then— and, yes, I can remember almost the exact moment when everything changed.

I had been having pretty severe stomachaches; so after some tests my doctor told me that because of stress, I had early signs of colitis. He said if I kept up my hectic pace, I might have serious medical problems. I went home that night really frightened. Knowing that my lifestyle was hurting my body, I feared for my health. And I was worried about *not* pushing myself so hard.

My wife and daughters must have been out that evening, because I remember wandering around the house alone trying to sort out what it all meant. Then I thought back to the last seat in the second row. I thought about the kids in that row, the kids I liked the most. I began to think, "What if I *belonged* in the last seat in the second row?"

They belonged there. So did I. What was so shameful about that?

I'll never forget that feeling. I sat down and felt . . . such *relief*. It had taken me a long time to discover that I not only *belonged* in the sixtieth percentile, but I was also happier there! Over the years I have learned that we humans tend to be happier when we are where we belong rather than trying to get somewhere that is not really who we are.

๛

Many parents have an absolute fear that their child will turn out to be nothing more and nothing less than average. And when parents say "average," it's as if it were a four-letter word. We try everything in our power *not* to let our children be seated in the middle. We don't want them to be "just" average.

When I'm talking to groups of parents these days, I often ask them to please remember the bell curve. "You know," I remind them, "in this entire room, with only two or three exceptions, we're all under the big hump together."

For the sake of all the kids (like me) who are under the bell curve, I'm just hoping that parents can accept that little truth. It's pretty good territory, there in the middle rows.

On the other hand, now that I'm a little older, I understand better why my parents wanted me to get into the first seat in the front row. They kept hoping that I would get out from under that bell curve. They worried about what would happen if I turned out to be nothing more than average.

Of course they had the best intentions. That's why parents worry. We want our kids to work harder, do better, so we plan more activities and lessons to fill up their "free time." What's too bad is that, in doing so, we create a world in which children are under tremendous pressure to excel all the time. Students in middle school are already beginning to put together their academic résumés for college. When children are pushed to excel, they never get to experience the wonderful lessons that are learned from failure.

I've ended up feeling a great deal of gratitude for my failures. Of course, there are people who don't believe me when I tell them I belong in the last seat in the second row. They challenge my position by reminding me of books I have written and the many wonderful accomplishments I've been fortunate to achieve. Over the years I have learned that there are some aspects of my humanity— perhaps my kindness and my ability to understand others—that probably belong in the first row. But there are many other aspects of Gottlieb that belong in the last row—technical skills, attention span, and memory (to name a few).

Overall, I'm comfortable here with my many friends in the last seat in the second row. If you ever get tired of trying to get ahead or if you feel lonely once you're there, you are always welcome back here. There's plenty of room, and we are pretty nice people.

It's fairly easy to guide our children to becoming the kind of people we think they should be. All we need is some vision, some recollection of our own experience, some vigilance, and our natural parental gift of lecturing. But it's a very different piece of business to help our children find the happiness that comes with discovering where they belong in life. For that, we need faith.

When I speak about having faith in our children, I don't mean faith that they won't fail—because they will. I don't mean faith that they won't make stupid decisions— because they will. I mean faith in their resilience.

Where does that resilience come from?

I once treated a patient struggling with loneliness who made a comment I have never forgotten: "I feel like my soul is a prism," she said, "and everyone I know only sees one color. But nobody sees the prism."

In a letter to my grandson Sam, I told him the wonderful Jewish teaching about the imprint that a child receives from God before he is born. After giving the unborn child all the wisdom needed to succeed in life, God puts his finger on the child's lips and says, "Sssssh." And at that moment, when we're imbued with knowledge, God forever leaves an impression on the upper lip.

So where does the resilience come from? It comes from the prism. From the wisdom our children have always had but don't *know* they have until they need it. From the imprint on our upper lips. And ultimately, resilience comes from the gift of life itself; we get wounded and then we heal. It's almost inevitable.

Listening—
The Great Healer

Amy is one of my dearest friends, and I've known and loved her nieces, Chelsey and Katie, since they were little girls. When Chelsey was about five years old and Katie nearly twelve, they would enjoy going for trips in my van. The two girls, sitting way in the back, would chat with each other while I drove. Until we arrived at our destination, they usually kept their own counsel. But occasionally, one or the other of them would pipe up and ask a question or provide some commentary.

On one occasion, just as we pulled up to a stoplight, I heard Chelsey's small voice coming from the back of the van: "Uncle Danny, what does *having sex* mean?"

I didn't want to answer. This was the kind of question she should be asking her aunt Amy, not me! Not here! Not now! But as my face reddened and my mind went into overdrive, I reflected that I was, after all, somewhat knowledgeable in these matters. Twenty years earlier, I had addressed questions about sex with my own daughters. And furthermore I was a psychologist as well as a good friend to these little girls. All I had to do was think developmentally and come up with an answer appropriate to Chelsey's age and experience.

I took a deep breath. And with a bit of anxiety and feigned confidence, I announced: "Having sex is what grown-ups do when they want to have a baby."

An adequate answer under the circumstances, I thought, and I was somewhat puzzled when it was followed by a very long pause. I figured the silence meant everyone in the back was satisfied with the answer. It was Katie, the older sister, who finally broke the silence. "Uncle Danny, what are you talking about? Chelsey just asked you, 'What does *heaven's sakes* mean?'"

"Oh," I said as I could feel the blood rushing to my face, telegraphing my embarrassment to the world (or at least the backseat).

And then Katie thought it would be a good idea to follow up: "Uncle Danny. What were you thinking about?"

In fact, Katie's question was exactly the right one. Something did get in the way of my listening, and it wasn't earplugs. I was so lost in my own thoughts when Chelsey asked her question that I could not hear it clearly. Thoughts literally interfere with hearing. Emotions like anxiety, insecurity, depression, and anger also impair it. Even positive emotions like elation and exuberance interfere with hearing. As the pace of life increases, so does the speed of thought. And so does the intensity of our emotions. When that happens, the chances of patient, thoughtful listening decrease. These days, when I'm talking to kids about their lives, what I hear more often than anything else is that they feel unheard and misunderstood.

We adults are living such fast-paced lives, we're so caught up in our own concerns and insecurities, that many times we don't even hear what our children are trying to tell us. Sure, we may hear the words, but too often we miss the meaning. One teenager described it as "drive-by parenting."

I know how my own anxiety—dating back to the days when I had so much trouble in school—got in the way of listening to my children. When my daughter struggled in school one year, it pushed all my buttons, reminding me of old shame and insecurity. With what I thought was concern for her, I pushed her to study more; we got tutors; and *her* mother and I checked homework even more carefully than usual.

Sure, I was mobilized because of concern. But the anxiety was about my history and not my daughter's future.

I see so many parents push their children relentlessly to achieve, ultimately because the parents are afraid of the future. One adolescent girl said to me, "Why does my mother mistrust me? When I bring home a B on my report card and tell her I did the best I could, she never believes me." But what if I could have managed my own anxiety so many years ago when my daughter was having trouble with her schoolwork? Maybe then I could have seen it as my daughter's struggle, and not mine. Maybe then I could have been more compassionate. Maybe then I could have had more faith that my kid would be okay.

Of course, listening is an issue between adults too, not just with children. "*He* doesn't hear me" or "*She* doesn't listen to me" are refrains often repeated in my workshops with married couples. At one of those workshops, I decided to ask the men and women to tell me about listening to another kind of voice—the one that comes from within.

"When you listen to yourself—your truest self—what do you hear?" I asked.

The women and the men in that group responded quite differently. Almost all of the women told me they could *hear* the voice but they couldn't *respond*. Many said they felt guilty or selfish, so they "kept it at arm's length." The men said they knew the voice was in there, but they just couldn't hear it anymore.

What happens when we can't hear our own voices?

A man in the group who had been a lawyer all his life said, "I'm successful by all measures." He had belonged to a powerful law firm, attained his career goals, and made lots of money. I asked him to tell me about his life. When he was a boy, his father had told him to make honor roll, and he'd done so all through high school. In college he consistently made dean's list, and in law school, following his father's advice, he made law review. Again at his father's urging, he joined a prominent law firm and made partner. "Here I am facing retirement," the man told me, "and I don't know whose life I've been living."

His own voice—the one inside—had been silenced. He had never listened to it, and now he didn't know where it was. And that's what happens: Over time, if we don't hear ourselves, our own quiet voice gets silenced.

If we want to hear our children, we need to take time first to listen to ourselves. Only then we can listen to them.

My most powerful lesson about listening came during the early days after my accident. I noticed that the more I simply listened, the more people spoke to me. And the more people opened their hearts, the more deeply I cared. I listened with an open heart, and people spoke with an open heart. How did this happen? Well, in addition to losing many functions in my body, I "lost" all of my personal pronouns. It was always about them—that is, other people—and their humanity. I had no responsibility to change anyone, only to listen and learn. And in the process, I discovered how to care deeply.

Holding My Mother's Hand

It was six o'clock in the morning on New Year's Day 1998 when I heard my father's frightened voice on the telephone.

"Danny, your mother's been rushed to the hospital. You'd better get here right away."

My mother had not been aging gracefully. She had been growing more and more frail and confused and gotten much worse in the two years since my sister died. With her health deteriorating, I expected that she would soon need full-time care. She argued about giving up her car keys and refused to allow us to bring someone in to help her bathe and dress. My father was exhausted trying to keep her safe. We faced the prospect of my mother going into a nursing home, which was awful for all of us.

I arrived at the emergency room at what is now the AtlantiCare Regional Medical Center a couple of hours after receiving my father's phone call. My father was crying. He tried to say, "Don't rush." The words just trailed off behind the tears.

Later, he would tell me what had happened. My mother had awakened in the middle of the night complaining of stomach discomfort. She paced their apartment for a couple of hours and then passed out on the sofa. The emergency van came quickly, but nothing could be done. My mother had had an aneurysm. She died shortly after the ambulance arrived at the hospital.

Just the night before that, I learned, they had been at a New Year's Eve party with their fellow seniors. I later found out that my mother had asked my father to dance with her. It was the first time in ten years that they'd danced together.

In the emergency room, a nurse met me at the door, expressed condolences, and asked me if I wanted to see my mother. Then the nurse led me to an isolated cubicle and pulled back the sheet so I could see my mother's face. From my wheelchair, I could see only some of her features, as they were only partially visible. I glanced quickly at her closed eyes and motionless lips before my gaze went to her motionless abdomen. I stared at it for a few seconds . . . just to be sure.

I guess time seemed to stop because I was jarred by the nurse's gentle voice: "Would you like me to place her hand in yours?"

Before this moment, I couldn't have imagined holding the hands of a corpse. But this was different; this was my mother.

As I stared at our hands touching, I reflected back over our lives together. Early pictures of my young mother show an attractive woman in the classic Lana Turner mold. She had jet-black hair that she dyed regularly (well into her seventies) and a dark, Mediterranean complexion. I recall the constant gleam in her eye and how she always seemed to be partial to feisty children.

Throughout her life, she had been a people magnet. People just seemed to be attracted to her. There were always visitors in our house, and wherever we went, people would tell me what a wonderful mother I had.

Frankly, I never really felt that way.

She was a fighter, and many of her fights had been with me. She pushed me, she nagged me, she annoyed me, and she often embarrassed me in front of my friends. And she didn't always trust me. Sometimes I thought she didn't trust me because she didn't understand me, and sometimes I thought she didn't trust me because she really *did* understand me.

Now, as I held my mother's hand, I thought about the kind of family she had created. I remembered how powerful I believed she was when I was little. After all, she could manage the family, help in my father's store, volunteer for several organizations, and solve whatever problems my sister and I had. And through it all, she had seemed fearless. If one of her children needed something, she would take care of it. Nothing stopped her.

But how well had I known her? What blinded me was that she was not a woman to me, not a *person*. She was a mother. Hope springs eternal, and I always thought that one day she would "get" me. But it seemed like she never did. She never got to know me, really, and I never got to know her.

Why did I battle with my mother? In part, I think, because she was always trying to get me to be different. She wanted me to be more married, or more successful, or more . . . well, whatever it was. And in hindsight, her wishes were not about me; they were about her. I recall a conversation a couple of years before her death when we had been talking about my marital status and I said to her, "Mom I want you to know something—that I'm a fifty-year-old man and I'm happy. I have a good life. I feel good about what I've accomplished. I have great friends and I feel like I've made a contribution to the world. I want you to know that about your son. I want you to know that you've contributed to that."

Her comment was, "Yeah, but you could be happier."

If I had been younger, I would have been angry at that comment. She *still* didn't get me! Instead, I felt sad. I knew, at that moment, she had never truly experienced the feeling of happiness.

All those years, we didn't get each other because we were trying to change each other. She was trying to make me into someone more accomplished, more healthy, and more happily married. I was trying to make her into someone more compassionate, tender, and insightful. Each of us was trying to make the other into the person we thought we needed.

Of course, both of us were clueless about what we really needed. But in our hunger to make things different from what they were, we became impaired. We didn't see each other for who we were . . . until the day she stopped breathing and we held hands.

Now, for the first time, I saw my mother as a woman of her generation. Born in 1914, she had dreamed of going to college, had even been offered a scholarship, but her family dissuaded her because girls didn't do that back then. Despite her disappointment, she had created a life that had meaning and dignity.

I recalled how well this woman had taken care of her own aging, frail mother who lived in our home. I remembered how she had always insisted the whole family travel every Sunday to visit her mother-in-law, who was widowed and living alone. I reminded myself how, despite being barely able to afford it, she had sent her two children to a private Quaker school for preschool and kindergarten because we were living in a community that was increasingly anti-Semitic.

She had wanted us to get a good start. Helping my father manage his Army-Navy store, she had made the business so successful that we could move to a middle-class neighborhood.

That's the woman I had not been able to see, because until then she had just been my mother—and a mother who was far from perfect.

I was looking at the motionless hands of two people who had loved each other for fifty-one years. She could no longer squeeze my hand, nor could I squeeze hers. And only now did I see her in a different light.

Now I understood that for all the times she fought *with* me, she fought *for* me even more.

I remembered my junior year in high school when I got A's and B's on my report card—with one exception, a C in Spanish. This was a big deal because I had never made the honor roll before. I'd never even come close. This time, I was more than close. I knew my Spanish teacher had made a mistake when he gave me that C, because I had gotten A's and B's on my Spanish exams that marking period.

When I argued my case with my Spanish teacher, he acknowledged his mistake, and he changed my grade to a B. Finally, I had made it—honor roll!

Three weeks later, I was called to the principal's office for disciplinary action.

The principal accused me of changing the grade on my report card. I said my Spanish teacher had changed the grade and explained exactly how it happened. The principal didn't believe me. My Spanish teacher apparently got nervous about the mistake he had made or, perhaps, about not following procedures in correcting my grade. Whatever the reason, he wouldn't take responsibility and let the principal believe that I had changed the grade.

Threatened with suspension, I tearfully called my mother. I was not at all sure how this would go. Whom would she believe?

My mother arrived at the meeting fifteen minutes after the principal's phone call, and she looked angry—but not at me! Turning to the principal, she looked him in the eye and said her son would *never* do anything like this. She knew the story, and she knew the Spanish teacher was lying. And she said, "You will not suspend my son from school for something he didn't do."

Holding my mother's hand now, I thanked her for that. And then I went on. I thanked her for creating a family where we could laugh at one another and at our own mistakes. I recalled how her hands had made me feel safe when I was little. I also remembered how, when I was a few years older, I rejected the security that her hands had offered, pretending I was more independent than I really felt.

How hard it was to pull my hand away from my mother's. It's always difficult to say goodbye to someone we have loved for a lifetime.

As I left my mother's side for the last time, I thought about the hundreds of relationships I've seen in which people love each other but cannot see each other clearly. They cannot feel the warmth in each other's hearts; all they can feel is resentment for past injuries, or fear of future ones. Or years of frustration as they have tried unsuccessfully to change each other. It saddens me to see people who love each other yet cannot open themselves and simply hold each other's hands.

Peace Talks

During an event that was meant to emphasize harmony in the Middle East, a cantor in our community made what I felt was a racist comment about Arabs. Outraged, I wrote an editorial for a local paper. I began the editorial with an old Jewish parable about a man who spread false rumors about his rabbi. Having decided that he wanted to acknowledge his wrongdoing and take his punishment, the man went to the rabbi and asked how he could make amends.

"Take a feather pillow to the top of a hill and shake out all the feathers, and then come back to me," said the rabbi. When the man returned, the rabbi said, "Now go back to the top of the hill and collect all the feathers."

"That's impossible!" the man protested.

"Precisely," replied the rabbi.

This is what this clergyman has done, I said in my essay. There are hundreds of ears that have heard his racist remark, and many of those ears belong to our children. The feathers can't be taken back.

After I finished the column, but before it was published, I sent a copy to the cantor. He and I went back and forth—nothing hostile, just exchanging e-mails. He didn't get the point I was making, and I didn't agree with the view that his remark had merely been taken the wrong way.

The final e-mail I sent to him was on a Friday. I wrote at the close of the letter, "Shabbat Shalom," a wish for peace on the Sabbath. In his e-mailed reply to me, he closed by saying, "We could all use some shalom." In his words I heard some human emotion. In a second, I wrote back to him and said, "Could we have lunch?"

I received a lot of letters about the editorial; almost all were negative. Then I got a letter from a rabbi who said, "You're right about what you said, and you're wrong for saying it. You've done the same thing the cantor has done. You've soiled his name in the community."

Was the rabbi right? I think he was—and I was humbled.

Some days after the column appeared, the cantor and I had lunch together. He talked about his life; I talked about mine. He talked about growing up in an Arab country and his dreams of becoming a scientist. I learned where his values came from and what he loved about being a cantor. I knew we would probably never be friends. But I also knew that I never would have written an editorial like that had I seen him as a whole person.

I had reacted to the cantor's words. But until I sat down with him and we talked and listened to each other, I *only* knew his words, along with the story I told myself about who he was.

The lesson I learned? If we want peace, we must be peaceful and not simply talk about it. If we want our children to be open and generous when they face their fellow humans, we have to model that. When I advocated for peace with a closed fist, as I did in that article, I had taken a selfish stand of righteous indignation. That never opens people's hearts. Just the opposite.

Everything began to change when the cantor said "we," opening the door to talk about us. Months later when I looked back, the world hadn't changed. I assume that the cantor hadn't changed either, and my life hadn't changed. But I learned a valuable lesson, and I feel more kindly to a man I judged harshly.

For a Change, Do Nothing

Max, a sixty-year-old tailor, follows a routine that hasn't changed in forty-five years. Every day, he puts on the same threadbare clothes and sets off for his shop. Along the way, he stops in at the synagogue to pray. After working hard all day, he returns home and hands over his earnings to his wife.

Max has only one little vice. Every day, he spends a dollar on a single lottery ticket.

One day, Max comes up with a winning ticket. He arrives home with a check for a million dollars. As usual, Max hands the check to his wife. The next morning, he gets up, puts on his threadbare clothes as always, and gets ready to go to work.

His wife stops him. "Max, you've worked so hard all your life and now you have the opportunity to enjoy yourself. Go get a new suit and a massage. Take care of yourself!"

Ever-dutiful Max does exactly what his wife suggests. He gets a massage and a facial, and then spends hundreds of dollars on a beautiful new outfit. It's a complete transformation. Who would ever believe this is the same Max?

He crosses the street with his shoulders back and chest out. Just then, a car barrels down the street and runs over poor Max.

Because he has been so good throughout the years, Max takes the express lane to heaven. He gets to talk to God directly: "God, I only have one question. I have been such a good person my whole life. Always, I'm the same Max, living the same way. Finally I get to be a different kind of guy, and you take everything away. Why?"

God pauses for a moment and says "Max, to tell you the truth, I didn't recognize you."

Many of us live our lives as though we would be happy with ourselves if . . . (just fill in the blank: More money? Obedient children? A perfect spouse? Better looks?). I know I did. As a matter of fact, this was one of my first observations about being human.

All my life, I never felt that I was good enough. My school performance, as I've mentioned, was not very good, and because of that I felt shame. And not only that, I was the younger brother of an extremely bright, attractive, popular older sister. Though I was popular enough, I always thought I was too short compared to other guys— and that bothered me. As for my shortcomings as a student, adults around me said that I was just lazy. I secretly thought that I must not be very bright—either that, or there was just something defective in me. So I never felt that I fit in with my super sister or my high-achieving friends. I secretly told myself that if I were taller, stronger, or smarter, I would be okay.

Later on, when I first began working, I told myself that if I received a great deal of professional acclaim, earned a respectable income, or married a beautiful woman, *then* I would fit in. Yet after I did all of these things, I still felt I didn't fit. So I worked even harder.

After I broke my neck—when I realized that *no matter what*, I would never feel like I fit in—I began to watch those people who appeared to fit in, as well as those who didn't. In my despair and loneliness, like a desperate child looking for his family, I hoped that I wasn't the only one who experienced life in the way I did.

What I observed was this: Most people appeared to be doing the same thing I had been doing—working terribly hard to become different or better.

Like the lesson learned by poor Max the tailor, change is not always good. Sometimes the greatest change we can make is when we *stop* trying to change ourselves. In her book *Radical Acceptance*, psychologist Tara Brach describes a middle-aged woman, a patient of hers, who was caring for her dying mother. When the end was very close, the mother looked in her daughter's eyes and said, "All my life I have felt there was something wrong with me. What a waste!" Recounting this story, Brach says, "It was as though the mother had given her daughter a final gift."

Most humans, I've noticed, are trying to figure out what's wrong and then change it. Whether our goal is to fix what we think needs fixing, to effectively hide our defect, or to finally find security or unconditional love, most of us work very hard to bring about change. And most of us, when we're not successful with that effort, do what I did: work even harder.

A couple of years ago I saw a man in consultation who had been in psychoanalysis for eighteen years. This man was in his mid-sixties and looked pretty dejected when he came to my office.

"I feel like a failure both as a man and as a patient," he told me. "When I first went into therapy, I didn't feel like I was very important in this world. And now, after all this work and money, I still don't feel like I'm very important."

In a light-hearted attempt to broaden his perspective, I said, "I have good news and bad news. You are not a failure. You are truly not very important in this world."

At first he laughed quite hard. And then he cried. And then he laughed again. He told me he cried with relief and sadness about all of the wasted time. And he laughed because deep down he *knew* he wasn't as important as he thought he should be, just as I, as a child, knew deep down that I would never fit in.

When we try to change ourselves, the focus of our worldview becomes narrower. The more self-critical we are, the more self-absorbed we become.

Most of us have a part of our brain that observes our own behavior. But the observers lodged in our brains are neither objective nor compassionate. They're more likely to be judgmental, always reminding us that we are not good enough. And so we criticize ourselves, judge ourselves, work harder, sleep less, or push our loved ones more . . . all in an effort to somehow be okay.

Most people I know assume that the judge is accurate! They consider it the "ego ideal"—the voice that tells us how to be the person we think we should be. Others call that critical voice the conscience. Generally that critical voice is seen as one who has power or wisdom.

I see it a little bit differently. What I've discovered is that the voice in the brain is *not* the voice of some wise observer. Rather, it's the voice of our own anxiety and insecurity telling us that if we become different, then we will no longer be insecure. I see that critical voice as a scared child saying, "*Do this* and *do that* . . . and maybe then we will be okay." Instead of taking that critical voice seriously, try listening to it as an anxious part of your personality that needs comfort and reassurance rather than obedience.

The truth is, if we become comfortable with who we are rather than who we think we should be, then we will be less insecure.

WHAT OUR CHILDREN SEE

Inevitably, when I'm talking with a group of parents, the conversation turns to stress. Most parents I speak with are overly involved with their children, making sure they are getting good grades and filling their social calendars with activities. Also, most of these adults complain that they themselves don't sleep enough or get enough downtime. When I ask them why they work so hard, the answer is always the same: "For the children."

The problem is, many children I have spoken with say they feel guilty about how hard their parents work. They tell me they try to perform the best they can so as not to add stress to their parents' life. So here we have two generations sacrificing themselves to take care of each other.

Armed with this information, I ask parents how they feel about their lives. Like their children, most complain. Some say they don't get enough sleep. Others say they have too much pressure to achieve and too much stress. But, like their children, the parents believe that if they continue on this path, it will lead to a better life "tomorrow."

And then we talk about what our children see when they look at us. We become their vision of tomorrow. And of course that's not what most of us want. We have other dreams for our children—that they will find comfort, peace, happiness, and serenity. But where are their role models?

Several years ago, a father called to ask if I would see his twenty-three-year-old son, Dwight, for consultation. The father, Bernard, was concerned because Dwight kept going to college and dropping out, getting jobs and losing them. Bernard reported that his son just seemed unhappy and directionless. I told the father that if Dwight wanted help, he could contact me and I would be happy to schedule an appointment. Several hours later, Dwight called.

When I saw him, I understood his father's concern. Dwight didn't look depressed; he looked more empty or sad. He said he wasn't happy with the way his life was going but didn't really know what to do about it.

When I took Dwight's history, his background seemed pretty uneventful with the exception of his parents' divorce, which had occurred when he was about ten. Since the divorce, Dwight said, he'd had a good relationship with both of his parents and there did not seem to be much conflict between them. In his youth there was no significant trauma, no history of depression from either parent.

I told Dwight that I was struck by the fact that his father made the initial call. Usually, the mother is the most concerned; she's the one who makes the first call to a therapist. So I asked him about his relationship with his father. In reply, Dwight told me that he and his father had always been very close.

"He was the one who would read me bedtime stories," Dwight said.

From the age of about seven on, father and son would go camping every summer. "I looked forward to those trips all year," Dwight said. "When I was about ten or eleven, Dad began to worry a great deal—first about how I was doing following the divorce. Then, several years later, he worried a lot about my adolescent sister who was becoming a handful. During that time, he also worried about his business. I still looked forward to our camping trips, and I knew how much he loves me, but he just never seemed happy."

I referred this young man to a good therapist who I thought would be helpful.

A week later, Bernard called and asked what I thought. With his son's permission to discuss his case with his dad, I said, "I think one of two things is happening. Perhaps your son is so worried about your unhappiness that he is afraid to leave you and start his own life. And there's another possibility. Like most children, he sees his future through your eyes. Without even knowing it, he may be assuming that his future life will look roughly like yours does today."

After several seconds of silence, Bernard asked, "What can I do?"

"The answer is simple and terribly difficult," I said. "You must fix your life. It is an act of love to your children to find meaning, joy, and contentment in your own life."

So what can we do to help our children look forward to a future filled with hope, true happiness, and gratitude? As I said to Bernard, we need to take care of ourselves. But how do we do that?

ꤷꕤꤷ

As a therapist, I have many families come to me with a child who is symptomatic—depressed, withdrawn, and angry. Though the parents may see the child as the "problem," I often end up working with the couple and not the child. And frequently as the marriage improves—as the couple finds joy and rediscovers their love for each other—the tension in the house diminishes and the child's symptoms go away.

This is the way it was with Jeff and Martha when they came to see me with their son Tony. He had been caught bullying other kids at school. The boy, eight years old, and a little heavy, looked angry and withdrawn. But one didn't have to look hard to see the sadness in his eyes. And I knew in the first session that his sadness wasn't accessible, because he didn't feel safe to open up. He expressed himself through bullying, but sat silent in the sessions.

As the parents talked about themselves and their children, I heard a lot about Tony's twelve-year-old sister, who seemed to get much of his mother's praise and attention. I began to get the picture of a marriage that had been strained for years. To deal with it, Jeff closed down when he came home from work. He didn't get involved in the family. He had become withdrawn and a bit depressed. Martha got over-involved with her children, especially her daughter. Feeling the anxiety, both parents tried to make everything "normal." So big issues didn't get talked about and, certainly, the pain felt by both parents never got acknowledged.

The parents, not the child, were responsible for the change in the family. When Jeff and Martha began to devote more of their energy to each other, to caring for their own lives, to giving voice to their pain and compassion to each other, I could see the change in Tony.

Jeff and Martha began going out on dates once a week. Then they took dance lessons together. And everyone seemed happier.

What changed?

We didn't try to cure illness. We tried to pursue happiness.

Our National Anxiety Disorder

❦

"Maybe all of life is about how we manage our anxiety," I once said to a friend. "Different people manage it in different ways, but it seems to afflict everyone." In 1999 I wrote a column suggesting that we were in the grip of an outbreak of a national anxiety disorder. Of course I didn't have a whiff of statistical evidence to support such a claim. What I did have were friends, patients, callers to my radio show, and my own experience.

In the late 1990s, public schools (especially suburban schools) were getting more competitive and more demanding. The pressure to get in to a good college—always a factor—seemed qualitatively different by the late nineties. Even kindergartens, some of my friends said, were getting competitive.

I also observed that during the nineties, anxiety about crime was high and one of the fastest-growing forms of housing was gated communities, yet violent crime was down. Financial anxiety seemed rampant, yet the stock market was booming.

As I say, that column was written in 1999. That was two years before we were all exposed to terrorism and our epidemic of national anxiety disorder soared out of control.

❧

Was I right in what I said to my colleague? Is life really all about *managing* our anxiety?

Consider this. People who are accused of being controllers do so because they have anxiety about being out of control. People who are compulsive about work, cleaning, alcohol, drugs, achievement, or anything else are exhibiting a form of an anxiety disorder. Insecurity is a form of anxiety; so is shyness. Marital arguments, road rage, interrupting people while they are speaking are all about anxiety.

Every year before Passover Seder I do some reading to make the holiday more interesting and relevant. In researching for my seder last year, I discovered that when Moses took the Jews out of Egypt, not everyone followed him. The article I read estimated that only 20 percent followed him, and the rest stayed behind. And why? The vast majority of us would prefer to stay in our day-to-day routine even if it involves suffering. And why? Rules, routines, and predictability are ways of keeping anxiety under control. The greater the anxiety, the more we cling to these things. Because change equals anxiety.

Which brings me to the profound parable of Moe, Larry, and Curly. (Any resemblance to my childhood heroes is purely coincidental.)

Moe, Larry, and Curly have been shipwrecked on a small island for years. One day, a bottle washes up on shore. One of the guys rubs the bottle, and a genie pops out. The genie says, "I've got three wishes, and since there are three men here, each gets one wish."

Moe, who happens to be Parisian, says, "What I wouldn't give to be with my lover in a little café on the Left Bank, drinking wine and watching people stroll by!"

Poof, he's gone!

Larry, a German by birth, says, "Ever since I've been here, I've kept track of every sunrise and sunset, counting the days to Oktoberfest. Oh, how I'd like to be in a beer hall in Munich right now!"

Kaput, away he goes.

Then the genie turns to Curly.

"What's your wish?" she asks

"You know," he replies, "I kind of miss those guys."

So there it is: Curly's wish is the same as that of the 80 percent of Jews who stayed in Egypt. To feel secure deep down, we want what we already have. Much as we complain about it, given the choice, there's a Curly inside who says, "Just give me what I had yesterday."

That's the beauty and curse of the human mind. The beauty is that we adapt. The curse?

Well, how do we get off the island?

My own anxiety has been a constant companion. And while I've never been able to banish it or even deny it, I recognize that my relationship to my anxiety has changed over the years.

Recently I went on a three-day meditation retreat. It was wonderful, relaxing, and centering. I arrived back home on Sunday evening around eight o'clock feeling extraordinarily peaceful. I unpacked and went to bed a couple of hours later. At two o'clock in the morning, I woke up with my chest pounding and horrible thoughts going through my head about work that wasn't finished, responsibilities I had taken on that I feared I couldn't complete, and on and on. My anxiety demon was back.

Once I realized what was happening, I said (almost out loud): "You son-of-a-bitch! I devote *three days* to calming you down and you couldn't even give me five hours in return!?" And then I laughed at the futility of trying to escape. Of *course* my anxiety was there. It always would be. Did I really think a three-day retreat was going to lock out my long-term companion? Silly me.

That's typical of what we do. We try to make bargains with our anxiety. We say to our anxiety, "Well, what if I achieve more—then will you go away?" Or, "What if I move to a gated community, where I'm safe from crime?" Or, "What if I make much more money—will you guarantee that I never have to worry again?"

Not long ago, a friend told me about a feeling he had—that he just had to work harder and harder to achieve some kind of security.

"I feel like my demons are nipping at my heels," he commented.

What could he do to prevent those demons from nipping?

"Sit down," was my response.

That really is not a demon chasing you. It's just a part of your own mind demanding attention. I believe true security happens when we are no longer afraid of our own minds. If you feel anxiety, simply feel it. If your mind has taken you to a dark place, just stay there.

I told my friend that there is only one thing to do when you feel like you are in hell: "Find the nearest bus stop and sit down." Responding to his dazed and confused reaction, I continued: "When we wait for a bus, we know it's coming, but we don't know when. It doesn't matter whether it's hot or cold, whether it's raining or whether you are in a terrible hurry, it comes when it comes." And when I suggested to my friend that he find the bus stop, I added, "because one day you will find yourself in heaven. And guess what, there is a bus coming there, too!"

That conversation made me reflect on the relationship I've developed with my own anxiety. After all these years, I can't shun it, deny it, or even manage it particularly well. Yet I do feel that my anxiety has undergone a change of direction.

Like most people, I was certainly afraid of all of the major catastrophes that can befall us. But as time passed, and I found that I had suffered many of them, I discovered that I felt less afraid.

I've developed faith (for now) in my resilience. I also have faith that at the deepest levels, when suffering returns, as it surely will, I will be okay.

Certainly, that faith does not make my anxiety go away. I still get anxious when my wheelchair makes a funny noise . . . or when I have this strange sensation and wonder if my catheter is leaking . . . or when I have to go to a meeting in the winter and wonder if anyone will be around to put my coat on. I also worry about my lectures and the words in this book, questioning whether they will truly reflect what's inside of me and whether the way I express myself will be of help to you.

So my anxiety and I still spend lots of time together. But our relationship has improved greatly. I no longer try to control it. And paradoxically, in the process my anxiety has less control over me.

THE GIVE-AND-TAKE OF CARING FOR OTHERS

At the tender age of twenty-four, my wife, Sandy, learned that she had malignant melanoma. My daughters were just one and two years old. I knew I had to "be strong" for them. I also had to be available for my wife, who was in terrible pain emotionally.

I couldn't miss too many days of work because I was the sole provider for the family. But in retrospect, I think I was going to work because I desperately needed an anchor—some predictability. Work felt safe.

In addition to caring for everyone, I also acted as the family switchboard operator. Nobody wanted to bother Sandy, so everyone called me with the same question: "How is she?"

We had to live with the consequences of the disease. My beautiful young wife not only had to deal with a life-threatening illness, she also had to cope with a leg that was deformed because of surgery. That was especially hard for a twenty-four-year-old woman.

Then there was the anticipatory fear of the sickness associated with chemotherapy. Five days a month, for one full year, we traveled to the Fox Chase Cancer Center in Philadelphia for treatments. After each chemotherapy visit, Sandy became more ill with nausea and fatigue. And with each successive visit, she anticipated becoming even more ill. Day by day, we lived with stress and exhaustion, and in the background questions loomed. Did it metastasize? Will it be back? Is Sandy going to die? And, meanwhile, our daughters needed our care.

I was beginning to learn what it means to be a caregiver.

At the time that Sandy became ill, I was doing postgraduate training in marital and family therapy. My supervisor was Geraldine (Gerri) Grossman, one of the senior teachers at the Family Institute of Philadelphia and a wonderful, compassionate woman. Supervision would sometimes get pretty personal because the unexamined emotions of a therapist inevitably have a big impact on therapy.

Sandy's cancer was diagnosed in the middle of my supervisory year. When Gerri asked how I was, I responded as if some automatic button had been pushed. I told her how Sandy was doing physically and psychologically, what was happening with the girls, and so on. This was "my story."

But she persisted. "No, I asked how *you* are. Not everyone else."

Initially her question disoriented me. Then, for the first time in months, I stopped worrying about everyone else. And sitting there in supervision with my teacher, I began to cry.

I was pretty surprised and embarrassed by what was happening to me; but I felt safe with Gerri, so I went on. I realized how tired and frightened I was. I saw I had been working too hard, pretending I was okay when I really wasn't. It was as if I didn't want to know those vulnerable feelings. I was afraid if they came out, I would collapse and not be able to do the job I needed to do.

I've noticed a few things about caregivers and those they help. Most work hard and pretend to be stronger than they really feel. Almost all caregivers feel lonely and misunderstood—less important than the people they take care of. The mantra I frequently hear is, "How can *I* complain? Look at what my loved one is going through!" And being a caretaker also means feeling guilty, helpless, and frustrated. It always seems that we are not doing enough to diminish our loved ones' suffering.

And caregiving is usually thrust on us by chance. One day we are living our lives, and the next day everything seems to be in free fall and we are responsible for holding things together. This job becomes ours whether the person we are caring for is someone we adore or someone with whom we've had a conflicted relationship.

Many caregivers are angry. Makes sense to me! Anyone who is exhausted is likely to become angry. Anyone who is responsible for a job they feel they cannot do will get angry. Many get angry at those they take care of. Many get angry because their support system is not as responsive as they need it to be. And many are angry because they feel the life they had yesterday has been stolen.

The person being cared for, whether a patient or a loved one, is often angry, too. After my accident, I hated being taken care of even though I needed it. And, secretly, I wanted people to take even better care of me. I wanted them to know how scared I felt and wanted them to hold me. I wanted them to know how overwhelmed I felt and I longed to hear the words "You don't have to worry about anything ever again. I'll take care of your life for you"—the same words that small children long to hear when they feel scared.

What I hated was being taken care of. It robbed me of my sense of independence and worth. Sometimes, it was more hurtful than reassuring to be taken care of by people I loved. That's because I knew that, more often than not, caretaking was taking something out of them. I felt guilty for being so dependent. And the more dependent I was, the worse I felt about myself.

I would say to my wife, "I'm okay. Go out to lunch with your friends or go away for the weekend. I'll be fine." But I was lying, and she knew it. So she also lied by responding, "No, that's okay. I'm really fine and I don't need to get away." So here were two people who had gone through terrible adversity, both lying to each other out of love! And both angry at everything that had brought them to this situation.

Anger can get caregivers to work harder and to move mountains. Anger has helped me pursue justice in an unjust health-care system. But anger can also be poison. Whether it is justified or not, over time, anger turns into bitterness and righteous indignation, and then we become poisoned with our own emotions. The poison of unresolved anger takes an even greater toll on the body than the job of caretaker.

Here's the problem. To have a chronic illness or be traumatized any other way is to feel alone and isolated in the world. And to be a caregiver is to have those exact same feelings. So, now we have two people who love each other and both feel alone, and neither one is open and honest with the other, making the alienation feel so much worse. How many tears we must have shed behind each other's backs!

What can be done?

When caregivers who are feeling burned out ask me that question, I first tell them about many wonderful organizations that provide respite care and support groups for caregivers. Organizations like the Well Spouse Foundation do a terrific job.

But there is another source of care for caregivers. And it can be life sustaining. If you are taking care of me and you love me, ask me what it's like for me to be ill and to be taken care of. And then just listen. And then—this part is very important—tell me what all of this is like for you. What are your losses and fears? Tell me about all of your mixed feelings and hopefully I'll be able to listen, hold your hand, smile, and feel deeply about your life. That will help you. That will help me.

If we wear kid gloves when interacting with one another, we will never get to make genuine contact with the people we love and need the most. When I look back, how I wish Sandy and I could have held each other and just wept about the terrible event in our lives instead of protecting each other.

In *Wounded Hearts*, Rachel Naomi Remen, MD, co-founder and medical director of the Commonweal Cancer Help Program, quotes a woman addressing the mother who has been her caregiver. The poem begins with a quote of her mother's oft-repeated advice. The response is that of her daughter. The poem has the title "Mother Knows Best."

Don't talk
about your troubles.
No one loves a sad face.

Oh, Mom.

The truth is
cheer isolates,
humor defends,
competence intimidates,
control separates,
and sadness . . . . . .

sadness opens us to each other.

Children's Dreams and Parents' Faith

❧

Your children are not your children.
They are the sons and daughters of Life's longing for itself.
They come through you but not from you,
And though they are with you yet they belong not to you.
—Kahlil Gibran, from *The Prophet*

When my nephew Billy was in college, he formed an improv comedy group that was pretty good. In fact, when he graduated, he continued the group, which began to get some notoriety performing on a number of college campuses. But despite the notoriety, Billy wasn't earning much from his improv activities. So I watched most of the adults in his family get frustrated and then critical.

I don't know exactly what the family's vision was for Billy's future, but my relatives certainly didn't relish the idea of him making a career of improv comedy. As for all the struggling he had to do to make a living, *that* was a piece of the family's nightmare—it was what everyone feared.

Then Billy got married. Family concerns escalated. All eyes were on this young, married man with a college education trying to eke out a living as a stand-up comic. At one family gathering, my father (Billy's grandfather) confronted Billy and told him, "You should get a regular job so you can support yourself and your new wife. Forget about this comedy stuff and do something that's more stable and predictable."

Ever the observer, I listened to what my dad had to say, thinking, "Okay, I can understand everyone's frustration. But I can also understand that this young man has a dream he feels passionate about, and he is pursuing it."

Then Billy said to my father, "But wait a minute, Pop-Pop. Are you saying you want me to get a job like the one you just retired from?" (My father was a businessman who had run a small Army-Navy store all his life.)

"That's right."

"But you were miserable in that job for thirty-five years! You said it was boring and you felt trapped but didn't know any alternatives," Billy replied.

My father reflected on his grandson's response, and so did I. At that moment, I recognized that my father was doing what most parents do. Automatically, we try to guide our children based on our own experiences. Often it is an effort to keep our environment stable. The guidance we give them is an attempt to allay our own fears and turn our visions for them into a reality.

So here was some valuable insight. At the age of twenty-two, like most young people, my nephew was confident he knew more about what would make him happy than the adults around him. But what made Billy unusual was that he was willing to take a great risk to pursue his dream. He was risking his family's approval to follow a path no one else before him had taken.

All young people have dreams, and many of those dreams are not consistent with their families' wishes and expectations. Some families will encourage their children to travel their own paths. And some families will feel anxiety and insecurity when their children begin to craft lives that are seen as "different."

Over the next several years, Billy continued to work with his improv group. He and his wife had a baby. And they continued to struggle financially. Finally prudence forced him to give up his dream and get a regular job—the kind he always said he would hate. But he surprised himself by liking his sales job. And given his improv skills, he was an excellent salesman. I suppose you could say that he "grew up"; but more than that, he simply grew in ways that his elder family members probably did not anticipate. If the whole family had sat down to chart out a career path for Billy, it never would have looked like the one that he created for himself. In finding his own path, he found a way to be happy with his life by following a course that none of us could have imagined. His family thought they knew what was right for him. They were wrong. Billy thought he knew what was right for him, and *he* was wrong too!

Daniel Gilbert, in his book *Stumbling on Happiness*, discusses the way people make decisions about their future.

Gilbert's research has shown that those decisions are usually based on what people *believe* will make them happy. But he has found that we're not very good at such predictions. And while we put a lot of effort into avoiding what we think will make us miserable, we are also pretty poor at those kinds of predictions as well.

Suppose someone had said to me, when I was thirty-two years old, "Over the next twenty years you will become a quadriplegic, your wife will leave you, and shortly after that she will die. And shortly thereafter, your sister and parents will die. But don't worry, you will be happy, anyway." Imagine what I would have thought.

But that's exactly what happened. And many people I know who have experienced great adversity have told me that the trauma did change their lives—for the better.

So we are pretty poor at predicting what's good and bad for ourselves and even less effective when we try to do it for others. One of the reasons we don't do it well, says Gilbert, is because we make these predictions based on our own past experience or what we have been told about the future by others. But that really doesn't give us much evidence about the future for ourselves, let alone our children.

The fascinating thing about my family was the way everyone tried to project into Billy's future and figure out what would make him happy. But no one could foresee what that would be. Not even Billy.

In the poem I quoted at the beginning of this chapter, Kahlil Gibran goes on to say,

> *You may give them your love but not your thoughts,*
> *For they have their own thoughts.*
> *You may house their bodies but not their souls,*
> *For their souls dwell in the house of tomorrow, which you*
>   *cannot visit, not even in your dreams.*

ABOUT COMPASSION

❧

Recently I was in a restaurant, having dinner with two couples I'd known for several years. The relationship between the couples went back a lot longer—about ten years. Though we started off on subjects of mutual interest, the conversation soon shifted to things that I wasn't involved in. Suddenly, my mind began to race and I thought, "I really don't belong here. They only invited me to be nice. I'm the fifth person at the table. That's a weird number. I'm all alone."

As their conversation continued, my insecurity grew. All of a sudden, I "noticed" I was having this intense dialogue inside my head. At that moment I said to myself, "I'm crazy now. I hate when this happens. I hope it doesn't last too long." I also realized that I was suffering.

I felt overcome with anxiety and loneliness, and I watched the process over the course of dinner as the intensity of these painful emotions ebbed and flowed. At certain points, I was in the conversation and at other moments I wandered back inside my mind. As the meal drew to a close and we said our goodbyes, I began to think, "Oh, no, I'm going home by myself now. That means I have very little distraction from these uncomfortable thoughts and feelings. I hope this doesn't get worse. But I'll certainly pay careful attention."

As I got in my van, those feelings stayed with me, but so did the awareness. And so did my compassion for myself. I knew I was feeling anxious and alone.

Now, the question is this: If I'm watching myself be crazy, *who am I?* Am I the crazy person or the caring observer of the crazy person? Who am I, really?

From my position as observer, I could see this was all the result of painful emotions that all of us experience at some time. And I knew it would pass. But in the meantime, what could I do for myself? How could I be more kind and compassionate to the crazy person at that restaurant table who had to get in his van and drive home alone?

For times like those, I have an exercise. First, I try to imagine the moment when Moses met God on Mount Sinai, as described to me by a friend in the clergy. He told me of one interpretation of that moment: There was an instant when God's back was turned, and as he passed in front of Moses, *just for a moment*, Moses saw the world through God's eyes.

Then I try to see the world through God's eyes—the eyes of a being that is loving, compassionate, and caring. Through these eyes I look at my family and feel compassion for them. Then I feel my heart expand. And if I can keep looking through those eyes of love and compassion, perhaps I can see the world and all its people as God sees them. And, finally, I try to see *myself* through the eyes of that loving, compassionate God.

As a matter of fact, sometimes in the morning when I wake up, I look at myself in the mirror and make compassionate eye contact. Sometimes I see an old friend, other times I'm sad and moved to tears. But it always feels intimate.

Back in the restaurant, the observer in me felt compassion and sadness for my suffering. If only we could always do that with ourselves and each other—watch and care. If only we could see the world through God's eyes.

WHOSE NEEDS ARE SPECIAL?

Some time ago, I got a call from a woman who wanted to know if there was a day-care center for people with disabilities. I was stumped. After a moment's thought, I had to tell her that I didn't know of one.

Her question made me think, though. If there was a Disabilities Center, who would be eligible to go there? Certainly, with my wheelchair I could get in. So could people with walkers or canes. I'm positive the Disabilities Center would admit people who are blind and those with a mental illness such as schizophrenia or bipolar disorder. People with developmental disabilities like autism should be allowed in, too. But then I considered people with learning disabilities, those who wear hearing aids, and those with glasses or with attention-deficit disorder. Then I wondered about the garden-variety neurotics like you and me. Would anyone be left out?

Clearly, it's not easy to say who is disabled and who isn't, or even what it means to have a disability. Just look at our language. We have gone from "crippled" to "invalid" to "handicapped" to "disabled" to "differently abled" to "special needs."

But "special needs" doesn't work either. Because you can see my wheelchair, it's obvious my needs are special.

But your needs . . . Sorry, they're just ordinary!

See what I mean?

Okay, so what are we talking about when we refer to the handicapped, crippled, disabled, or those with special needs? I think I can bring some clarity to all of this confusion. Gottlieb's definition of disabled is: "To have something other people don't want." If you look at someone and think to yourself, "I'd never want to be like that! No way!" I'll bet you're looking at someone who's disabled. (I understand that could include many other things such as poverty, but give me a little slack here: After all, I am a person with special needs.) And you have that reaction because the people with disabilities look strange, act strange, or worse, are dependent on someone else.

Most humans, I have observed, treasure their independence. When they look at someone who has become dependent, the reaction is, "I'd never want to be like that." In intimate relationships, "dependency" is now used almost like a curse word. So, afraid of acknowledging our dependency, we create a new word . . . "interdependent." Because of our invisible dependency, we are—I am—what most people fear.

The problem, of course, is that whether or not you're disabled right now, you're on your way to joining our ranks. Disability-rights activists call the nondisabled "temporarily abled." With aging, inevitably, comes the loss of physical and often mental abilities. The process usually begins around age forty when we buy our first pair of reading glasses. Then, by fifty, some of our memory starts to go. We all move toward a part of our lives when we're going to be more dependent.

And here's a bit of reassurance. You'll get over it.

How do I know that?

Because that's what we humans do. We get over things. Even things that seem like our own worst nightmares.

Several years ago, I saw in therapy an obese man who was in his late sixties. Because of the weight he carried, his knee joints were beginning to fail. He already had one artificial knee. At the end of our consultation, he labored to get out of his chair. It took him several minutes and, frankly, it was difficult for me to watch him suffer.

He finally stood up, took a breath, and looked down at me. "This might be inappropriate to say, Dan," he said. "But as hard as it was for me to get up, when I look down at you, I think, 'Thank God I can get up!'"

"Well, this might be inappropriate to say back to you," I responded, "but when I watched how hard you worked, I was thinking, 'Thank God I won't have to go through all that crap when I get older!'"

I got insight into the process of becoming more dependent when I was reading *Tuesdays with Morrie,* by Mitch Albom. When Morrie, the author's mentor, was first being affected by ALS (Lou Gehrig's disease), he turned to Mitch and said, "Oh my God, one day somebody will have to wipe my ass."

When I read that quote my immediate thought was, "You'll get over it, Morrie. I did." Having a catheter and needing someone else to bathe and dress me used to be a horrible indignity. Now all those things are simply regular parts of my life, just as anyone who needs to wear reading glasses or bifocals makes a habit of putting them on and taking them off. Whatever you need today that you didn't need yesterday simply becomes part of your life.

You see, people look at me and imagine themselves in my position and feel fear. I certainly did that when I was younger. Because of my disability, I have already experienced what most people will as they age. I consider myself very lucky as I listen to my middle-aged fellow humans worry about their losses. All the stuff they fret about now, I already have endured, so I don't have to be concerned. That frees my mind up to worry about all sorts of other things!

And speaking of having a mind—that is the thing that affects how we age more than anything else.

Here's what I mean.

From the time I was a boy, I studied how my father aged. First I watched as his hair changed color from brown to pale brown to gray. Then he lost all his hair. In later years, he slowly lost his hearing, his stamina, and his sense of taste. Losing those things didn't seem to bother him much, but some other things did. When he was in his eighties, my father used to say, "I'm ready to leave this vale of tears."

One day I asked him if he was really in so much emotional pain that he was ready to die.

"Some days I am," he said.

"So tell me about those days, Dad."

"Well, I get thinking. I buried my wife and my daughter. And I think of my only child struggling every day in a wheelchair. Those days I'm ready to die."

"But Dad," I said, "those things are true every day. What about those days you are not ready to die?"

He thought about it for a minute. "I guess I'm not thinking about those things on those days."

So that's what's coming up, I thought. As we get older, we'll have days when we might rail against our losses. Other days we won't even think about them. Some days, the dependency and the indignities will seem too much to bear. Other days, those drawbacks won't make much difference—we'll be pleased to be alive. And those perceptions can change hour by hour.

Sound familiar?

That's right. No matter what our age, we'll still think the way humans think and feel the way humans feel.

No wonder there is a little comedian inside of me who finds great humor when people unthinkingly say to me, "Sometimes when I think about my life, I just feel paralyzed." I just look up and say, "Sometimes I feel that way, too!"

THE LIGHTER SIDE OF DEATH

Several years ago, Maiken Scott (my radio producer at WHYY) and I decided that we would do a radio show on death and dying. There was a woman at the University of Pennsylvania Hospital who was terminally ill, and she volunteered to be on our show. So Maiken and I, along with a sound technician, went to the cancer ward of the hospital for the interview.

The ward reeked of illness, chemotherapy, depression, and despair. It was sterile and eerily quiet. Jane, the woman in the terminal stages of cancer, was curled up in her bed. Because her peripheral veins had collapsed, she was receiving chemotherapy through a catheter in her neck.

Our audio equipment was minimal. We had only one microphone (you know, it's listener-supported public radio). When I do interviews in a situation like this, my ears are alert to the slightest sound because I know the microphone is sensitive and will pick up extraneous noises. Having the same concern, Maiken sat very close so she could move the microphone between the bedridden Jane and me in my wheelchair near the head of the bed.

So there were the three of us, all crowded in together. We talked for about fifteen minutes—about this woman's life, her family, and the onset of the disease. Finally I moved to the more difficult questions. I asked Jane what it was like to be dying. I asked whether she was mourning her own life.

Knowing that was a powerful question, I was prepared for the reflective silence that followed. But during that moment of silence, I heard water dripping. Fearing that the *drip-drip-drip* would be heard on the audio, I turned as best I could to look in the bathroom. The sound didn't come from there, but I still heard it clearly.

That's when I looked at the floor right under my wheelchair. A puddle was forming. Because we were all so close together near the head of the bed, Maiken's knee had knocked my catheter off the connection. Urine was dripping on the floor.

Now I don't know about you, but I've never read any etiquette books that explain what you're supposed to do when you're in the presence of someone who's terminally ill and your catheter is leaking on her floor.

In that silence, I said, "Jane, I hate to mention this to you now at this moment, but I think I just peed all over your floor."

Maiken looked dazed at what I had just said (she frequently has this response to the things I say).

Jane replied, "It's okay; don't worry about it."

"But I'm terribly embarrassed that this happened," I said, "and that it happened now."

Again Jane reassured me. "Don't be embarrassed, Dan."

And I said—almost not believing I was in such a playful

mood at this moment—"Since I'm embarrassed and you're not, can we say that you did it and I didn't?"

"Sure," she said. And we all laughed.

Later on, when the nurse came in the room, I said, "Jane did it!" And we all laughed some more. Twenty minutes later, when I resumed the discussion, there were tears in the room.

Laughter in the face of death is not possible if we don't face death openly and honestly, with an open mind and an open heart. Almost everyone facing death has great fear and confusion and sadness and aloneness. But so many people live their lives without facing what's happening!

We are anxious about death because we feel out of control. And we are anxious about death because we love life. I don't think anxiety about death is the problem. *Denying* our anxiety is a problem.

I was fortunate to have a father who didn't try to deny death. And because of that, he taught me a lot about dying. I watched him die with grace, with dignity, with comfort. I felt love for him, of course, but I also felt such gratitude and awe for the way he died. I felt gratitude for his teaching. I felt gratitude that, up to the final days of his life, I could kid around with him.

Just imagine my gratitude when I found out I could keep on kidding him even after he was gone!

Dad always wore a watch. As he aged, he became compulsive about checking the time. Every couple of minutes, it seemed, he had to glance at his wrist.

After he had retired, this habit of his became fertile

ground for teasing. "Come on, Dad," I'd say. "How come you're looking at your watch all the time? What's the rush? What—do you have a big meeting coming up?"

Finally I asked him, "Hey, Dad, what would happen if I stole your watch?"

He gave me a baleful look, glanced down at his watch (it was still there!), and said, "I guess my head would explode."

After my father died, I visited the funeral home where I was given his personal effects. It took me about an hour to drive home, and it wasn't until I got to the house that I realized his wristwatch was among the items that had been carefully packed away and given to me by the funeral home director.

No, that's not right! I thought. *You can't bury Dad without his watch!*

Without a second thought, I turned around and drove all the way back to the funeral home. The director seemed surprised to see me back so soon.

I held up the watch. "My father would want to be wearing this."

The director led me into the room where my father's casket was being held and raised the lid. He lifted my father's lifeless hand and strapped the watch around his wrist. But just as he was about to close the lid again, I noticed something else that didn't seem right.

Someone had placed a *kippah*—the Jewish religious cap—on my father's head! Now this was a problem. My father had been a passionate atheist all his life. He wanted *nothing* to do with religion and never wore any of the traditional Jewish garments. This was the first time I'd seen him in a *kippah*, and I knew he would not be pleased.

I hesitated. Okay, Dad wouldn't want the *kippah*, so we will just take it off. But then I started thinking, "What if the atheists are wrong? What if there really is something there that rules and decides and judges and gets pretty mad sometimes?" What should I do? Do I honor his wishes, or do I avoid some potential serious risk? All this passed through my mind in a second or two. But the bottom line, voiced to the director, was, "Better take it off."

"Are you sure?" asked the director.

"Yes," I said.

So the watch was on, the *kippah* was off, and Dad was oblivious to the services I had just rendered him. Still, just after the director left the room, I couldn't resist a final remark.

"Okay, Dad. You owe me one for that."

I don't think Dad taught me *everything* I know about being a wiseass; he just made it easier because he giggled at all of my jokes. But I do know he taught me a great deal about dying well. I learned that, right up to the last moment, one of the things we're teaching our children is how we deal with this anxiety about death. Our progeny are watching and listening to us.

Despite his easy access to laughter, my dad was kind of a cynic about life. So when we both found out that he was at the final stage of his life, I wanted to know how he felt about the experience.

"When you look back over your life, Dad, what kind of grade would you give it?" I asked him, hoping it would be as high as a C.

After a few seconds of reflection, he said, "I think I would give it a B."

I was pleasantly surprised by his answer, happy to know that he'd enjoyed his life. And then, when I visited him a couple of months later (about two weeks before he died), he said spontaneously, "You know that question you asked me before about grades? After I thought about it for a while, I think I would give it an A."

Forgiving

When I first had my accident, I felt total rage toward the truck driver who caused it. I used to have fantasies of being able to take a baseball bat and break his neck and make him a quadriplegic. I nurtured those fantasies for a long time.

Our natural reaction to injustice—to any kind of injury—is anger. Anger serves us well. It mobilizes the fight-or-flight reaction, which helps us survive. And it protects our wounds. When we clench our fists, close our hearts, and defend ourselves against further injury, our resentment and anger become like a scab, protecting the tender wound from infection. But if the scab stays too long, the underlying wound can never heal.

Everyone is injured in life. The injury can be simple injustice—having a strict and unreasonable parent, for instance, or growing up with an aggressive sibling. Or the injury can be deep, hidden, and festering.

Years ago, I worked with Cheryl, a woman who had experienced horrific abuse at the hands of her father. What he did to her was heinous. He threatened her with violence, and then forced her to sit in a chair and bear witness as he beat her brothers brutally. Her story, as she told it, had such a powerful impact on me that I had to stop her two or three times during the telling, just so I could try to fathom what she went through.

When we next met, I did something that I rarely do in therapy: I asked Cheryl what the previous session had been like for her. And part of the reason I asked was because I wanted to talk about what it had been like for me.

Cheryl replied, "It's the first time anyone has been willing to smell my emotions."

We talked about what happens when you keep hatred and resentment locked up inside. For years, Cheryl had thought she was hiding the abuse. In the beginning, she was. But hidden away, it atrophied and decayed. The resentment began to rot and stink. And now that was just what she was carrying inside—not just the memory of the abuse, but all the feelings of rage that were layered on top of that horrendous experience. Over time, it took on the odor of decay.

This child who had lived in that hell closed her heart in order to protect it. When she felt safe enough, she felt rage at that man. The rage gave her the illusion of power. She told herself, "If I hold the hatred, if I keep my fist clenched and my heart closed, I'll be protected." And she had spent thirty years protecting that tender part.

Given the horrific nature of her father's actions, there was no need for Cheryl to reconcile with this man. But for the last thirty years, she had been suffering with this terrible resentment. So what could be done?

Webster's defines forgiveness as "letting go of resentment." Simply that. It has nothing to do with the other person.

What's locked up inside of Cheryl is a suffering child. That child never received compassion, certainly not from either one of her parents, but not even from herself. She could never really connect with her suffering. She had to close herself off from it. As I had learned in my own experience with rage, it's very difficult to feel such hatred in your heart and feel compassion for yourself at the same time. When Cheryl could start to feel compassion for the child she was, for the woman she had become, then perhaps she could mourn her losses and feel deeply all that pain. That would be a beginning.

When Cheryl's father was hurting his children, he wasn't even aware that he was doing this to human beings. He didn't know about the humanity of his daughter and sons. And he still might not. Could this woman, his daughter, find the humanity in him? As she learned about his life, she learned about his own suffering, his blindness, and why he had attacked her and her brothers. She found out that her father had watched as *his* father beat his mother and then frequently had beat him, too. His abusive father had left the family when Cheryl's dad had been twelve years old. As she came to recognize how her father had lost his whole family when he was a boy, Cheryl tried to imagine what it would be like.

As these complexities came out, Cheryl's world turned less black and white. When Cheryl felt safe enough to open her heart and feel compassion, she no longer had a perpetrator and victim, villain and victim, or monster and victim. Now she could see how one human could harm another. She still had not condoned her father's behavior. But in making him human, she took away her father's power.

Forgiveness has nothing to do with reconciliation or even holding a perpetrator harmless. Forgiveness is the process of giving up resentment or anger toward another person.

There is a Buddhist story about a monk who was robbed at gunpoint at a bus station. Immediately after that encounter, he felt great fear. Moments later, he felt great rage at the perpetrator. These emotions continued to wash over him, and by the time he got home he was crying. When the monk told his student this story, the student said, "After all you've been through, why are you crying?" The monk replied, "I realized that if I had been raised by that man's family and if I'd had his experiences, I would have been the man with the gun."

THE GIFT OF HOPELESSNESS

I remember saying to my wife, Sandy, when she first arrived in the emergency room after my accident, "I've been hurt real bad and I am never going to get better."

I cried for a long time. In all of my despair and powerlessness, I needed options. So I told my loved ones that I would live with this for two years. And then I would decide whether I could go on or not. Having that option gave me the illusion that I had some control over a life that felt out of control.

At the end of two years, I took myself into the bedroom and I had a deep, reflective conversation with . . . well, I don't know. God? My god? My own truth? Anyway, the conversation went something like this:

"Okay, I will live with it if you give me hope that one day I'll walk."

And what I heard back was, "Nope. No hope. Live or die. Make your choice."

So I said, "Give me hope that I won't be so sick." (My health was so fragile—I just wanted some assurance that I would feel stronger and be able to fight off infections.)

And I got the same answer. "Either live with it or don't. It's not going to change."

For every request, I got the same answer.

That moment didn't produce great insight—insight came later. At that moment what I felt was more like confrontation and confusion. The little voice inside said, "Oh, shit, what do I do now?"

The two years were up; I'd tried to make a deal, see a way out, get some promise of hope—some tiny assurance that something would get better. But of course there were no promises. No hope. And I still had to make my choice.

I chose life.

I didn't choose life because I'm a hero. In fact, at first I was quite sure that if I'd had the courage, I would have taken my life. Then I told myself I chose life because of my children. But now I know, in hindsight, I believe I chose life because that's what we do. Given a choice, we choose life.

That was my great insight. But when I look back, there was another that was at least as important. And that was the gift of hopelessness. I never would have chosen the life I had if I'd reserved some hope that one day I would have the life I wanted. When false hope was removed, I chose the life I had.

Trust me. This great wisdom never would have come if it had not been preceded by my "oh, shit" moment. I think that's true for many of us. We have our moments of great despair. We ask ourselves, "How am I going to live with this?" Only later, if we are fortunate, do we come to understand that there is no hope to reclaim the life we had yesterday. This moment, and its aftermath, is actually the truth of our lives.

∾∿

I've treated many people who faced despair, and many who have avoided facing it until the last possible minute.

Harold was a very physical man who enjoyed skiing, hiking, and remodeling projects around his house. When he came to see me, he had been living with back pain for several years. Despite the pain, he lived his life fully. But the pain was getting worse. He saw several doctors, many of whom recommended surgery. He did a great deal of research, exploring many other options, before he decided on surgery.

Almost immediately after the surgery, he saw that his pain was diminished, but he had lost mobility in one leg. His surgeon said it was caused by swelling around the spine, and as the swelling diminished, Harold would probably regain function of that leg. His internist agreed with the surgeon. So Harold was advised to get a brace for his leg, to walk with a cane, install railings, and cut back on some activity. But he did none of those things because he still had hope that his life would be just the way it had been before.

Trying to resume his usual physical activities, Harold fell several times. He got frustrated. Every time he went to the doctor, he was told, "There is still a chance." But meanwhile, Harold was getting more depressed.

Finally, Harold's internist said to him, "If you haven't recovered your function by now, you probably won't."

All hope removed, Harold felt the despair that had

always been lurking inside. And that was his "How am I going to live with this?" moment.

But, Harold told me, he actually felt relieved when his doctor removed hope. In the absence of hope, he was able to mourn his loss and face his future. His great insight? He realized he didn't have to wonder how he could endure his physical restriction. He already knew how. He had been living with it for eighteen months. And now that he had stopped fighting, he could get the supports he needed to make his life easier. He told me he learned about his resilience and he also learned that having hope could be good news or bad news.

Several years ago, I treated a woman named Caroline who had been diagnosed with metastatic cancer. In that first moment after she heard the diagnosis, she said, she felt two things: "First, I felt blinding terror"—*oh, shit!*—"and then great clarity about what I wanted from my life. I knew I wanted to spend more time with the people I love, and I didn't want to work at my job anymore."

For the next six months, she told me, she struggled with the "How am I going to live with this?" question. She did so by aggressively attacking the cancer and traveling around the country to get different opinions. In the process, she was still able to retain her job but not able to spend much time with her loved ones.

Finally, after a visit with her doctor where she learned that despite all the treatments her cancer continued to spread, she gave up hope. Like Harold, and like me,

Caroline lost any expectation of ever reclaiming the life she had yesterday. But with that came her great insight—now she was free to live the life she had today. She quit her job, spent more time with the people she loved, and was even able to devote some time reading to children at a neighborhood day-care center.

Hope is always about the future. And it isn't always good news. Sometimes, hope can imprison us with belief or expectation that something will happen in the future to change our lives. Similarly hopelessness isn't always about despair. Hopelessness can bring us right into this very moment and answer all of life's most difficult questions. Who am I? Where am I? What does this mean? And what now?

What I've Learned About Heaven

◈

I knew there was no cure for my paralysis. Nor was there any cure for my baldness. But this was an infectious-disease doctor on the other end of the line, and he was calling me about my urinary tract infection. We had always cured them in the past, and even though this one seemed much more difficult than the others, I assumed we would resolve it, too.

So I was pretty shaken when he said, "I don't think we can cure this one, Dan."

Urinary tract infections are an inevitable side effect of spinal cord injury because the bladder is paralyzed. Ordinarily, I get a few infections each year, and after a couple of weeks of antibiotics, I'm okay. But this one had lasted a full year. I even told friends I was going to take my infection out to dinner to celebrate our first anniversary!

That moment on the phone, with tears in my eyes, that joke didn't seem so funny. After some research, I found out this was not an imminent death sentence. It did mean, however, I would have to take antibiotics for the rest of my life or else I could get quite ill. And of course long-term use of antibiotics is rarely good news for one's body.

That phone call represented a new chapter in my life, one that I was in no rush to begin.

❧

I do believe in coincidences, and I was involved in a quite a fortunate one when my friend Amy came over to visit just two days before that phone call. At one point, she asked if I believed in heaven. Without giving it any thought, I said, "Yes. You're in it right now."

I saw the dazed look on her face that I often see when I make proclamations, so I went on: "What were the chances of that sperm fertilizing that egg and producing your life? And what were the chances that you would have lived all the years you have lived in relative good health? And what were the odds that you would have so many people in your life whom you love and who care about you? And what were the possibilities that you could look out of almost any window and see the beauty of nature? Heaven? You bet."

Of course, my version of heaven is not the perfect one we read about in mythology or that many believe in. There is great pain and suffering and loss in this particular heaven. But deep inside, most know it—heaven, life—is precious. It just takes some careful noticing.

Margaret knew how precious life is.

I met Margaret, a woman in her early sixties, in a couples group. She had cancer. When first diagnosed, she was extraordinarily aggressive about getting treatment. She went to numerous doctors for consultation and did as they advised—following treatment, changing her lifestyle. As Margaret's condition deteriorated, she began to understand she was dying of the disease. She and her family called a hospice. It was an acknowledgment on the part of all of them that she probably had no longer than six months to live.

She seemed to be okay with this. Almost from the beginning, Margaret had been reflective about her life, and when the medical evidence made it clear that she was going to die fairly soon, she stopped fighting. Both she and her husband seemed at peace. They wanted to maximize the time they had left—not by going on vacation but by reading together, lingering over meals, going on walks. They knew their days together were precious.

When hospice care began, a representative was sent to meet with the family. On the appointed day, the hospice worker met with Margaret, her spouse, her three children, and a few neighbors who were close to the family. Shortly after that, I visited Margaret at her home. The disease was taking a toll on her appearance. Her complexion was ashen, her eyes had sunk in their sockets, and her hair had turned limp and colorless. But as she told me about the hospice meeting, her eyes burned brighter and an almost angelic look came into her face.

"I left the meeting to go to the bathroom," Margaret recalled, "and on the way back from the bathroom, I passed the laundry room. I saw someone had folded my laundry for me!" Margaret smiled. *"Aren't I a lucky woman?"*

Indeed. She is lucky to know that she's lucky.

If we don't have death, then we can't have life. We can't understand what it means to live.

We work so hard to avoid death because life is precious. That is why we clutch to this life so tightly. That's why we have so much anxiety, even anger, when something threatens us or our loved ones. But here's the contradiction: If you work *too hard* to avoid death, then you're not going to have time to feel how precious life really is. You won't be able to feel it. You'll know it in your head but not in your heart.

During a recent vacation, I had the good fortune to visit the Grand Canyon. I'm not a good enough writer to describe the magnificent vistas. Suffice it to say that when most people see it for the first time, they are moved to tears. Not from sadness, but from awe.

At the end of the day, several hundred people gathered to watch the sun dip slowly behind the canyon. Everyone sat in silence as nature did what it does. And in the moment the sun closed the day, everyone applauded. More awe.

And then I thought: But the sun sets every day, everywhere. And it is no less magnificent wherever it sets. The only difference here was in the attitude we all had as we watched.

When Is the Dawn?

More than 90 percent of Americans believe in God. But which God? To some people, God is the one we read about in the Bible, a male who can love and can judge harshly. He's lethal with his anger and pays attention to our every move. Others believe God is always compassionate and loving, a kind of perfect parent. The sign on the church around the corner from my house says GOD IS LOVE and perhaps that's true if we reverse the order. Maybe when we *feel* love, that *is* God.

There is a sacred Jewish prayer that contains the phrase "God is one." Perhaps what that prayer means is that when many come together as one, we find godliness.

What do I believe? It really varies, depending on the day. But today, I believe everyone has a piece of the divine inside. That gives us the ability to love others selflessly, to experience the feelings of humility, gratitude, and awe.

There is another Jewish teaching that says when we die we must give God an accounting for all of life's pleasures we did not partake in, God's attitude being, "Hey, I built that beautiful Grand Canyon! Why didn't you *at least* go take a look at it?"

So with that gift of divinity comes a responsibility. We should notice and care for the beauty around us, knowing that we are part of it.

Some time ago, I wrote a letter to my grandson, Sam, in which I tried to tell him about my sister, Sharon, who died before he was born. As I wrote the letter I was feeling her loss again, not only my own loss, but also the loss of a relationship Sam could have had with her. In that letter I wanted to bring her back in whatever way I could so that Sam could get to know her. So I told Sam about my eulogy to my sister.

I started to write Sharon's eulogy when we heard the diagnosis telling us she had only a few months to live. As Sharon got closer to death, I found I couldn't even read the completed eulogy to myself without crying. And I wondered how I could ever say those words to a public audience next day without breaking into tears.

Then came the day of her funeral, which five or six hundred people attended. When it was my turn to speak, I wheeled down the aisle, turned, faced all those people and, without crying, I told them a lot about who Sharon was to me. I told them she had become my dearest friend and confidante, that she had always been my role model for what it means to be devoted, to have integrity. I told them that in my lifetime, no one had ever understood me and loved me as well as she had, and that her loss would create a permanent void in my life. I also reminded them about the many causes to which she had devoted her life—that she was a passionate supporter of Israel and the freedom of oppressed Jews around the world. She had devoted much of her energy and resources not just to women's rights but to making the world a more just place for all of us. My sister, more than most, understood the tale of the Hasidic rabbi.

An old Hasidic rabbi asked his pupils how to tell when night ended and the morning began (which is the time for certain holy prayers).

"Is it when you see an animal in the distance and know whether it's a sheep or a dog?" asked one pupil.

"No," the rabbi answered.

"Is it when you can look at a tree and tell whether it's a fig tree or a pear tree?" asked another.

"No," the rabbi answered again.

After a few more tries, the pupils asked, "Then tell us, what is it?"

"It is when you can look on the face of any man or woman and know that they are your sister or brother. Until then, it is still night."

Our Orphanhood

Recently I was in the waiting room of a doctor's office where two or three people were sitting quietly reading their magazines. After a while, a middle-aged man came in the room and sat down, releasing a deep sigh that broke the silence. As usually happens in these situations, no one looked directly at the man when he sighed, but I'm sure the other people in waiting room noticed as much as I did.

Some time went by, and then the man sighed again.

At first, I had thought that sighing was an expression of emotion—perhaps sadness, anxiety, or stress. And then I realized that sigh was much more than I thought it was. It was a social expression. The man in the room was expressing those emotions to us. He was trying to tell us something about himself.

And I speculated about what would happen if we had all been listening attentively and he had permission to tell us about himself. What would he say? How would he explain what was going on in his heart and his head? And what would have happened to all three of those isolated people in the waiting room? Would we, somehow, have felt more connected?

A great thinker once said, "The divine child is always an orphan." I spent most of my youth and young adulthood feeling that and trying to repair it by trying to be a better or a different person. But it didn't happen. The part of us that is our soul is always an orphan.

For better or worse, our family probably gives us our first sense of who we are. Later on, we realize that our family can tell us where we come from, but no one can tell us who we are or what's inside of us. We ache for an understanding we can never have.

Feeling that fundamental aloneness as a boy and a young man, I thought if I did something differently I could fix it. And then, when I became a quadriplegic and realized it could never be fixed, the pain was almost unbearable.

Over time, I learned to tolerate the feeling that, in a way, I would always be alone in the world. Neither my parents nor anyone else would fully understand me.

Then I discovered something very interesting. I wasn't the only one who felt that way. I met people who had closely knit families, social connections, who were part of real communities or participants in a congregation with a shared faith, and even with all this apparent "connectedness," there were parts of their being that felt motherless, fatherless, and exquisitely alone.

And now, as I look around at my fellow humans, listening to their sighs and their words, I see that people inevitably feel the pain of loneliness. And so many of us humans do whatever we can to diminish that pain. I feel great compassion for people's longing, and I feel a deep connection to them. At our core we are all so similar. That's the dance I've observed of being human. We ache to be understood, to be seen for who we are. It's a fundamental of life. And at the same time, there is a part of us that knows we can never be fully known. It is one of our primary fears. If I open myself fully, how can I survive if I'm rejected?

In one of his monologues, the comedian Jackie Mason is talking to his psychiatrist. "What does a psychiatrist do?" The psychiatrist answers, "I'm going to help you learn about your unconscious." To which Jackie replies, "My unconscious is none of my business!" It's funny because it's true. That door never opens all the way. Because of that, there is a barrier between us and others. Most of us are never fully known, even to ourselves.

But there's also a sad part to the joke. When we close off part of ourselves, we lose a way to connect with others. Part of our journey, as I see it, is about opening little by little, at first to ourselves and then to others. Yes, we are orphans. But the more we unfold, the more connected we feel.

When I think about how this can happen, I vividly recall an interview I had with author Kristina Wandzilak on my radio show. Kristina had just published a memoir called *The Lost Years*. In the book she chronicled her descent into drug addiction, which began at the age of thirteen. For the next ten years, she lived on the street, was raped, and sold her body for drugs.

When I interviewed Kristina, she was in her mid-thirties. Toward the end of the interview, I asked how she felt about her husband reading such graphic details about her past. She told me how, for many years, she had lived in fear of what would happen if someone discovered her dark side. "I was always afraid that if he discovered my deepest secrets, he would leave me," she said of her husband.

Kristina told me that as her husband read the manuscript, she could feel her heart racing with fear. She felt as if she were literally baring her soul, letting her husband see parts of her that he had never seen before. Would he still love her after reading all that? Or would he be repelled?

When he was done, Kristina's husband greeted her with tears in his eyes. He said to her, "I love you even more now."

I thought about the great risk Kristina had taken. Few of us dare to expose so much, and all of us are afraid that our hidden parts will prove to be unacceptable and unlovable. Even when we hear the words "I love you," deep down we are saying to ourselves, "But if they only knew!"

I live alone. The vast majority of the time, I am not lonely. Sometimes I am. What's the difference? I could speculate about the factors that contribute to my lonely days, but I'm not sure that guessing would be helpful. After all, it could be an ache for someone or something I am missing, or it could simply be that I am a bit low on serotonin that day.

So when I feel lonely, I do what I have been doing for twenty-seven years. I notice. I am aware that I am suffering and I simply feel what I feel. That's all. It doesn't feel pleasurable. Like all other emotions, it passes. But if I were to fight with it, feel sorry for myself or be angry with the people who are not calling me, or grasp for relationships, that loneliness would stay much longer.

Often, when I finish meditating, I see a squirrel outside my window, and I see what we two have in common—this life force, this activity to pursue some kind of security, to stay alive. Sometimes I feel such an integral part of the universe that I can sit comfortably in the orphanage. I feel love, I feel part of something much bigger. In those moments I can connect with something that feels divine—either inside of me, or in the orphanage, or beyond—I don't know, I don't care. But when that happens, I don't feel alone.

An intimate relationship with a loving God can help diminish the aloneness for many people. But even without the religious element, feeling connected to the larger world can do the same thing. If you could pay close attention to the world's living force around you, eventually you would begin to see yourself as part of that world. And perhaps you could expand your sense of belonging to your fellow orphans. You could hear their sighs, feel sad, and not be afraid.

LOVE IS NOT ALWAYS PRETTY

After I broke my neck, I was in the hospital for more than a year. When I finally returned home, I hoped that Sandy and I could resume something that resembled a normal family life. But during those first couple of years, there were times (far too often) when we would make plans, then have to call them off because I was too ill.

I remember the day we had all been invited to a pool party. Ali and Debbie were very excited. We all got in the van and started out; but before we had gone very far, it became apparent that I wouldn't be able to go on. We would have to turn around and go back. Consumed with disappointment, Ali burst out: "I hate you, Daddy, for breaking your neck and ruining my life!"

I cried. I felt that I *had* ruined her life.

It was only later on that I realized what a remarkable thing my little girl had said. She had felt safe enough to be open with her fury. And, like most parents, I knew that I loved her enough to handle it.

When children are young, they inevitably utter the words "I hate you" for some injustice we've perpetrated. If we can tolerate our children's anger and have faith that it's temporary, they can feel safe when they have strong feelings. Sure, we might want to teach them how those feelings should and shouldn't be expressed. But our love is a container that's big enough to allow our children to express them.

I felt anxiety and concern later on when, as adolescents, my children launched into all sorts of risky behaviors. What was more difficult than showing my concern was admitting to the anger I felt. It wasn't anger toward them, exactly. But deep down I felt rage for what my own children were doing to the very children I loved so much.

During their adolescent years, when they were getting in so much trouble, I thought I was just being a protective parent trying to take care of my children. I was too scared to even realize the issue was my life as much as theirs.

Somehow, intense anger at our children seems dangerous and impermissible. Confident parenting doesn't seem to have room for feelings of helplessness, confusion, and impotence. And certainly most of us don't give ourselves permission to feel rage toward our beloved offspring. But the love we feel for them has to be big enough and secure enough to safely hold all of these uncomfortable feelings, theirs and ours. And that's a very big container.

At one point, the behavior of my eighteen-year-old daughter, Ali, was causing me all kinds of anxiety. I was afraid she was out of control, and I knew *I* felt out of control. I loved her and, at the same time, I was so frightened and distressed, I could barely feel my love and admiration for this child. All I could feel was anxiety and anger. My heart felt closed, and I didn't want her to know that.

I could barely tell myself that . . . let alone my precious daughter. What's more, our relationship felt like it was in a pretty fragile position and I sure didn't want to risk alienating her. (I found out years later that no matter what I did, our relationship was never fragile in Ali's mind.)

I struggled with these feelings and was terribly uncomfortable with the negative ones. But I was soon to be reminded that feelings always have a way of expressing themselves.

One weekend when Ali came home for a short visit, she noticed that there was a big, framed picture of her sister, Debbie, in the front hallway. A short time before, the parents of one of Debbie's friends had offered to have that picture blown up and framed, and I'd proudly hung it in the front hall. This was the first time Ali had been home since then, and it was the first time she'd seen the big, framed portrait of her sister. Ali's picture was there, too, but it was much smaller.

It just so happened Ali was in a mood to confront me about this. "Hey, Dad. Why does Debbie have a big, picture in the front hall and I don't?"

Without even thinking, I said, "Because these days she's a good kid and you're a pain in the ass! Next week, maybe you'll have a big picture in the front hall, and she will be the pain in the ass."

Ali laughed and said, "I know I'm a pain in the ass."

My words were playful, but when I heard myself, I knew those were the feelings I was struggling with. At that stage of my life as a parent, Ali was making me feel frightened and impotent. Debbie gave me safety. I hated the way Ali made me feel. But when she laughed and acknowledged how difficult she was, every fiber in my body wanted to take her in my arms and tell her how much I adored her.

I also realized, at that moment, that my deepest wish was for her to reassure me that she would be okay, that she would care for herself during this stage of life, and that she would be back when she was done. In this way, I needed her to take care of me because I was so frightened. Regrettably, I didn't have the strength or the clarity to tell her that, until many years afterward. A decade later, Debbie's portrait has been replaced by a framed photograph of Ali and her business partner that was on the cover of a veterinary magazine last year.

Another time my anger was turned on Debbie. But on this occasion, my awareness came to me in a dream.

After my divorce from Sandy, Debbie spent much of her time at my house while Ali spent more time with Sandy. All of us were devastated, and I was trying to maintain normalcy. For me, that meant going to work every day just as usual, but making sure I got home early each day to spend plenty of time with Debbie. Whatever time and energy she needed, I tried to provide. I was exhausted at every level.

One evening when I came home, Debbie was watching TV. I asked, "How are you?"

Debbie began to cry about how hard her day was, and I simply didn't have the energy to be compassionate. I listened, said a few words, and tried to listen some more.

But it was hard to hear her. Despite how hard I was working, I felt like I had been failing to protect my child. And like most humans, I don't like feeling like a failure. As soon as I could, I told her how exhausted I was and went to bed.

That night, I had a dream that Debbie and I had both done something wrong, and we had been sent to prison. In the dream, I got out of prison and she didn't. I went on with my life while Debbie stayed locked up in a cell.

When I woke the next morning, the dream was still with me, and I realized what it meant. I had put Debbie in prison so I wouldn't have to take care of her anymore. Encapsulated there was all my aggression toward her—for exhausting me, for stimulating those difficult feelings.

That told me about my anger. I could have had a dream in which I put Debbie in some place where she was surrounded by beauty and comfort, but I didn't. Instead, I had left her in jail. And her real crime? I guess it was exhausting me. Despite all my love for her, and all my hope of relieving her pain, I was angry at my helplessness and impotence. And I held her accountable (as my dream reminded me) for making me feel that way.

But here's what's curious about my dream about Debbie and—earlier—my sarcastic words to Ali. It didn't take me long to realize that the container of my love for them was big enough to tolerate my rage and helplessness. Yes, there were moments when I saw how I could rage at them for all that they could take away from me—the same kind of rage they felt toward me when I had my accident. And then I understood that our love for one another was big enough to tolerate rage and frustration and tears. Our love for one another is not always pretty. Gandhi called love "the prerogative of the brave," and it does take courage to open to the possibility of being vulnerable, being wounded, and being very afraid for ourselves and for those we care about. Love can sometimes be complicated and confusing. It's not always warm and secure. But it's always intimate and fundamental—the very fabric of our lives.

FAITH

At a lecture I gave for a group of young people, I told them I had recently read that only 20 percent of the Jews in Egypt followed Moses to the Promised Land. One young man immediately responded, "That's great, but what happened to all those people who left Egypt? They all died in the desert!"

Well, he was probably right. Certainly most of them died, including Moses. But I challenged him, "And who wound up in the Promised Land? Of course, it was their children. Those twenty percent who took a leap of faith may have done so because of the larger picture. They were thinking of their children, their people. They saw themselves as a small part of something much bigger."

At a very difficult time in my life, right after my sister, Sharon, died, I had a dream in which three men appeared and produced a mink-brown butterfly.

They said to me, "This is your soul. In order for you to become a complete person, you have to inhale this."

In my dream I looked at them and said, "I can't do this. It's a living butterfly."

"You must, if you want to become whole," they said.

I put the butterfly in my mouth. It started to flap around and I quickly pulled it out again.

"I *can't* do this! I might choke—I might die."

"That doesn't matter either," they replied. "You must inhale it to become whole."

So I took a deep breath, and when the butterfly reached the middle of my throat, I woke up.

That dream made me wonder where my faith comes from. When the three men asked me to inhale the mink-brown butterfly, I challenged them and refused, fearing for my own life. So when I finally took it in, what was that? Blind faith? Simply believing what they told me to do, obeying their command?

That's not what it felt like. Instead, I felt like I was letting go. Inhaling the butterfly was impossible. It was something I thought I could not do. It might cost me my life. But in my dream, after I challenged the three men, I began to let go, to take in the butterfly, no matter what the consequences.

Later, I thought, that's exactly what we have to do. To become whole, we need to integrate our divinity with our humanity, and that requires a leap of faith. And in that leap of faith, the ego might die. The butterfly might be more important than all of our theories, everything we believe in, even our identity.

Where do we find the faith to take such risks? I think we are born with it. Consider the faith of infants and children. They have unquestioning faith that they will be looked after and preserved from harm. Of course, that confidence gets eroded with time and experience, and that's when children begin to look for something they can plug in to—a cause, a religion, a system that will rescue them from anxiety and insecurity. As humans, after all, we look for respite wherever we can find it. The wisdom is in there—it's inside us. Can we trust it? If we don't trust the faith that comes from within, we trust external sources of faith in our pursuit of comfort as a way to keep our demons at bay.

Debbie taught me a great deal about inner faith—hers and mine—when she was twenty years old and a sophomore in college. That was a time when it seemed all of the trauma she'd lived through came home to roost.

Frankly, deep down, I had started to become concerned about Debbie when she was in high school. She had lived through her mother's cancer, her father's quadriplegia, and great stress and confusion in the family. Shortly after her mother and I were divorced, Debbie went through a time when her mother became extremely erratic and unreliable. And throughout all of this, Debbie kept up the appearance of the "perfect child."

Then she went away to college, and that all fell apart. Her roommate called from school saying she was concerned about Debbie's behavior. Debbie came home. She decided to take some time off and live at home while she did an internship in Philadelphia. She began hanging out with a crowd that, to me, looked dangerous.

As things continued to unravel, I expressed my concern to Debbie and told her I wanted to help her. Like most young people, she resisted at first, trying to reassure both of us that she was okay. But as things got worse, one day she looked at me with tears in her eyes and said, "Daddy, I feel like I am a diamond inside of a malignant tumor."

At that point, almost thoughtlessly, I did what almost any parent would do. I mobilized all the resources I could muster to destroy the tumor. During the year that followed, I dragged Debbie around from pillar to post. I sought out the best therapists and doctors, asked their opinions, all in search of the "right approach." As Debbie returned to college for her sophomore year, it was with the knowledge that I would continue to do everything possible to help her.

Then I got a call from Washington D.C., where she was going to school.

Debbie asked if we could meet at a rest stop on I-95. We set a time, and when I arrived, she was there, sitting on a bench by the restaurant. I felt a wave of concern—she looked so tired and unhealthy!

But she was strong enough to take my hand in hers, look me in the eye, and say, "You've done everything you could to help me. I appreciate it. But now my life is in my hands."

And I cried. I cried from sadness and helplessness and fear and, yes, from relief.

Driving home, feeling this great grief, I was reminded of what she'd said a year earlier about the diamond in the tumor. When she said, "My life is in my hands," I knew that was the diamond speaking. And I knew that my job as a parent was to always see the diamond—to have faith that it was there when I couldn't see it or hear it. I needed to nurture it, listen for it, and hear its voice under the chaos.

Our society is fond of slogans like, "Be all you can be." I'd rather we said, "Nurture the diamond." It's not about achievement. It's about blossoming and becoming.

In the words of my twenty-year-old daughter—her assertion that her life was in her hands—I heard something very similar to my confrontation with God: Live, or die. Debbie knew she was suffering, and she also knew that what she and I were doing wasn't helping. She knew that to survive, she had to take her life in her hands. And she had to decide to decide—just as I had decided—whether to live or die.

Just like me, and just like most humans, Debbie chose life. And in that moment, she didn't know what it meant or what it would look like or how it would unfold. That choice was a leap of faith. It was a commitment to live *her* life—not the life she was "supposed" to live, but her very own life—did more than anything else to nurture the diamond.

It's the same path followed by Moses: "I'm going to take this step of faith and go where it leads me."

In Pursuit of Peace

Just before a recent Christmas season, I found myself facing the prospect of writing a newspaper column appropriate for the season of peace and goodwill. It was a daunting task, considering that we faced ongoing conflict throughout the world along with fear of terrorism, political instability, and insecurity in our daily lives. With so much religious-based conflict in the world, I turned to the words of a peace advocate who became the world's symbol of nonviolence, Mahatma Gandhi: "We must be the change we wish to see in the world."

Why, I wondered, do so many of us work so hard all week in the pursuit of some type of security, and then go to our houses of worship for a couple of hours on weekends and pray for peace? What would happen if, for ourselves and our children, it were the other way around?

Those questions became my topic.

In cities, towns, and suburbs all across the country, we work very hard in pursuit of a sense of safety and security. We want to make things better for our future—our children's and our own. Some of us work eighty hours a week or even more to achieve as much as we can or maintain what we have. As we push our children to excel in everything they do, turning our backs on their stress (and ours), we try to achieve professional and economic security. In our relentless pursuit of that, we all seem to be suffering.

Yet when I ask people to stop and reflect about what they ultimately want in life, most answers are the same. They want peace. World peace, peace at work, peace in their families and inside their souls.

This is the confusing part. We work so hard for the things we think will bring security but we take a passive approach to the peace we want most desperately. We pray or wish or hope for peace. And when we do take an active role in pursuit of peace, it often produces the opposite.

Looking at the world stage through the lens of human history, the pursuit of justice through aggression rarely leads to peace. It just leads to more injustice.

Almost every day in my office I see families and couples who fight with one another in the misguided pursuit of marital or personal justice or equity. They believe that if they find justice, they will then be at peace. So we see a wife trying to convince a husband that he needs to spend more time at home, help out more, because she believes the relationship would be more balanced. *Then* there would be fairness. *Then* she would be at peace—so she thinks, anyway.

Of course, he has the opposite demands and often feels that if she stops nagging and accepts him for who he is, there will be peace. And the fighting continues, all in the misguided pursuit of peace through justice.

As with the fighting couple, I think we tell ourselves that peace will finally come when others change. And how do we expect them to change? By finally hearing our arguments. Or having some great insight. Or succumbing to aggression. But how can those be ways to achieve peace? Trying to change others is about intolerance, which is at the core of so much enmity. We cannot find peace unless we are trying to help others find peace also. It doesn't come when we win battles; it comes when we stop fighting.

So why not pursue what we really want—to be with those we love, and find more time for joy and rest? If these are what we want, here's where the change can begin. One of the things I ask people at my lectures to do is spend twenty-four hours without sharing a word of gossip. Don't say anything negative *about* anyone, and don't say anything *to* anyone that has the potential to hurt them. Do that for twenty-four hours and see how you feel at the end of the day. "And," I say to my audience, "please trust me: At the end of that day, you have been a peacemaker."

It might be an interesting way to become the change that we wish to see in the world.

WE, THE WOUNDED

People in America don't seem to like themselves
very much. How can you not love yourself when
you have a Buddha nature inside?
—The Dalai Lama, quoted by a follower
on one of his first visits to America

When I was in college and graduate school, I was taught how to diagnose people's symptoms or their "mental illness." I learned the labels. When it came to diagnosing, I could hold my own with the best of my peers. Maybe I still can. But that didn't help me become a therapist. Everything about psychotherapy I learned later, when I learned about wounds and the way our bodies and minds go about healing them and how relationships can help or impede the process.

When we are wounded physically or emotionally, everything our body or spirit needs for healing is focused right on the wound. That tender point of injury needs protection. So if it's a physical wound, the cells in our body go to work and form a scab that covers the skin to protect it. The psyche forms a scab, too—though of course it's invisible to the naked eye. The scab on a wounded spirit might be anger or resentment. It might be withdrawal or even depression. According to Chinese medicine, we have a heart protector—the necessary ingredient that protects our tender heart from injury. But the wound is still in there.

If all goes well in psychotherapy, those are the wounds that have a chance to begin healing. How? In their own time and their own way.

Hippocrates said that inside every patient is a doctor who can heal him. Gottlieb would add, "There's another side to that. Inside every healer is a wounded patient who needs care. And unless all four of us are present, there's a lie in the room."

Some time ago, I attended an advisory board meeting at the Center for Mental Health Services, one of the many agencies of the Department of Health and Human Services in Washington, D.C. Seated around the table were about thirty prominent national and international experts in psychiatry and psychology representing a vast amount of accumulated experience in providing mental health services. Included were department heads of a number of clinics and hospitals.

As at most of these meetings, the language used by the experts was bureaucratic. They referred to doctors and therapists as "providers" and to patients as "consumers." The discussion focused on what consumers want or need.

I had been hearing this language for months, and it always troubled me. So at this particular meeting, I finally spoke up and asked the people around the table, "What do you mean by 'consumers'? Why are you talking about *them*?"

I asked by show of hands how many people in the room had *not* wrestled with depression, or did not ever experience obsessive anxiety. I wondered aloud how many of them had never seen a therapist and been "consumers" themselves. I'm sure my popularity plummeted as soon as I asked the question. But as we looked around—and at each other—I knew my point had been made. Just a few hands were raised.

Clearly there was no "we" and "them." We had met the patient and he was us. We could not pretend that this was the kind of relationship where providers (us) were at a great distance from consumers (them).

As therapists, we have to have faith not just in the perfection of the people we're with, but in the process. Healing is partly what we do. Only partly. New techniques and short-term psychotherapies are very effective at changing symptoms, and I recommend them to lots of people. But what heals a wounded soul is *who we are* as much as *what we do*. What heals is our humanity and not our technology.

In therapy, as in any relationship, we need balance, integrity, and honesty. I think about my addendum to Hippocrates's statement, and I know that there is, sitting across from me, a person who is wounded and a person who is healthy. I sit with my patients knowing that they can contribute to the meaning of my life in a very large way. In return, I offer them companionship and compassion during a rocky time in their lives. I also offer them a heartfelt desire to understand their lives, a commitment to sit with them through whatever comes up in their lives or in mine. If my life is about understanding what it means to be human, those people I work with are my trusted teachers.

It's my responsibility to ask the questions that will open doors inside of them that maybe have never been opened. And I also want them to understand that the person they are working with may be both a good therapist (on most days) and a very wounded one. The title on my business card doesn't say "psychologist" or "family therapist." Under my name it simply says "Human." And to me, that is the work of psychotherapy: to help people understand and grow comfortable with their own humanity.

At an important moment in her own therapy, Ruth, a colleague of mine, observed that "psychotherapy, as a spiritual process, is not about concepts or techniques. It's about who we are with each other, therapist and client, alike."

Ruth wrote these words shortly after she had come to see me. I remember the session. She talked about many things—wanting more peace and happiness in her life, wanting her daughter to have less stress, wanting less conflict with her ex-husband. In the session I felt how much pain she had endured and I could almost feel her tender, wounded heart behind the "protection" of grasping and desire. Because I could feel her suffering, I felt great affection and sadness for her. And I knew that it was the desire itself that actually interfered with the natural healing process.

As Ruth was leaving, she paused at the door. I said, "Expect nothing."

When I uttered those words—spontaneously—they came partly from my wish to end her suffering and partly from a selfish attempt to communicate how deeply I cared for her at that moment.

And how did she take those words? Her first response, she wrote later, was a sarcastic one. "Expect nothing? Sure, me and the Dalai Lama!" But later on she reflected, "The words were bouncing around in my brain like a Zen koan. They are with me still, unsolved, yet penetrating though layers of my being."

A friend of mine who had been in long-term therapy said to me one day, "I quit therapy."

When I asked why, she replied, "Because I do feel better about myself. I'm seventy percent better. And I'm tired of going in every week and talking about what's wrong with me."

That says everything about psychotherapy. Many people have the belief that if we talk enough about what has wounded us, the pain will eventually go away. It's not like that. We can't keep picking at the scab and expect the wound to heal. The scab needs to come off, and then we need to have faith that the wound will heal itself in a healthy environment.

What's a healthy environment? In therapy, we're talking about a relationship where there's trust in each other, where we have compassion for each other. The relationship is terribly intimate and also has boundaries. The therapist has faith in the wholeness of the person sitting across the room. When the patient has faith in the process, he or she doesn't need to pick at the wound. Faith creates a place in which the wound can heal on its own.

WHAT WE LEARN
FROM OUR KIDS

I once saw a bumper sticker that said MENTAL ILLNESS IS INHERITED. YOU GET IT FROM YOUR KIDS. Sometimes I think that may be true. But the opposite is also true. We can learn great lessons from our children.

When my daughter Ali finished college at the age of twenty-two, she came home with her boyfriend, Geoffrey. This was a boy she had been dating since high school, and his family lived about a mile away. Ali and Geoffrey went to colleges that were several miles from each other, and I knew they spent weekends together. I also knew they planned to move in together. But now, Ali was asking the question that fathers—especially single fathers—never want to be asked.

"Daddy, can Geoffrey sleep over?"

I looked at her—dazed. A thousand thoughts went through my head in the next two seconds. I thought about integrity, right and wrong, and hypocrisy. I kept looking at the empty bed next to me, hoping her mother would reappear with an answer. In just an instant, I tried to sort out all my warring thoughts and come up with an answer. And failed.

"Ali," I said, "this is the first time I've raised a twenty-two-year-old, and I have no idea what I should do."

"Thanks, Dad," she said. "That's all right. I'll take care of it." Geoffrey slept over that night, and, not surprisingly, everybody was okay.

Children are wonderfully adaptive. Like most parents, I used to worry about what my young daughters could deal with. Then I found out they could handle much more than I gave them credit for. They taught me in small and big ways about adaptation, healing, and devotion.

After my accident, I was in the hospital for many months. When I finally returned home, my daughters would come to my bedside to see me. They were both little, and in my bed-bound state, I worried about them seeing my urine bag. I didn't want the girls to be exposed to that. Before either of them came into the room, I would make sure the bag was covered with a blanket.

After a while, I became more casual and stopped trying to hide the bag. Anytime they came in, they could see it alongside my bed. I knew they noticed it, but nothing was said. I had no way of knowing whether it bothered them or not.

One morning when I woke up late, Ali was already in the room. She was sitting by the bed, peering at the urine bag. As my eyes opened, she looked up. "Daddy," she said with a note of wonder, "you peed your *brains* out last night!"

Both of my daughters have taught me so much about adaptation. Debbie, as an infant, sat on her mother's lap when Sandy went through chemotherapy for cancer. To this day, Debbie is afraid of vomit and germs, but she has grown into a wonderful woman who has become one of the best mothers I've ever had the honor to witness. She has found great love and joy. Over time (and many packs of antiseptic wipes), the wound has healed and scar tissue remains.

Ali's childhood was filled with animals. She trusted animals more than people, because animals never hurt her and people did. When she was two years old, her mother was out of commission for a year with cancer; when she was five, her father was in the hospital for a year. So despite or because of these injuries, she has become a highly respected (and very empathic) veterinary nurse.

If I could have protected them from many of the things that happened in their childhood, I would have. They were injured terribly by illness and loss. When they were in their teens, their parents divorced. Yes, my children were scarred by the trauma, and to this very day my heart hurts because of it. But they didn't break.

I never would have chosen such a childhood for Ali and Debbie. But, sometimes, what looks good and what looks bad might not be either. We just don't know.

These kids have taught me they're on their own paths—not mine. And what a delight to watch them! (I know I really would *not* have enjoyed watching them follow my path, because I've already seen that movie.) I get a thrill every time I get to consult with Ali about my (or my animals') medical problems—or have Debbie review the rough draft of a newspaper column I might be struggling with. I take great pleasure in the way the balance of care and responsibility in our relationship is slowly shifting. I still worry and care for them, and they now do the same with me. And I take great delight in scaring them with my behaviors—as I did when I visited Israel at the end of the Intifada, or took a helicopter ride over the Grand Canyon. I tell them I do these things as payback for all of the things that they did when they were adolescents. (Their new mantra is, "Remember, Dad, just because you *can* do something doesn't mean you *should*.")

Yes, there was much suffering in their childhood, and I was unable to make everything right for them. But I have learned something from my own inability to protect them. In the way they have adapted and survived, they have taught me something about love: that love is easier when we have faith in our children's resilient spirit.

Rules of Parenting
Adult Children

My oldest daughter, Ali, put her beloved dog Morris to sleep a couple of weeks ago. Morris was an incredibly sweet dog and a devoted companion to Ali for nine years.

Ali doesn't have human children. She has animal children. And she is as loving and devoted a mother as you could imagine. So when Morris began to deteriorate, her grief began to well up, and so did mine. Because this dog felt like a child to my daughter, his loss had special meaning for me also.

I felt terribly hurt and protective of Ali, but her style of mourning is very private. She closed down. I spoke to her once as Morris was nearing death, and the pain my child felt was palpable. I asked if she wanted me to come to her house to keep her company, and she said she would call if she wanted me to. A couple of days later, when I called, I found out that Morris had been put to sleep a couple of hours earlier. Ali was crying. She was about to take his remains to be cremated. Again, I offered companionship. Again she declined. A couple of days later I checked in with Ali, and she said she would rather not talk about it.

It's so hard to watch my child suffer and not be able to put my arms around her and let her cry on my shoulder like she did when she was a child. When she was a little girl and that happened, we both felt better. But now, only I would feel better. I had to love her the way she wanted me to love her. This was about her needs, not mine. Yes, it was hard.

But Gottlieb's rules of parenting adult children are pretty clear: Respect their integrity and their authority over their own lives. Have faith that whatever we would want to tell them, they already know. Help is to be offered with an open hand. And the offer of help should always be in the form of a question: "Would you like . . . ?" or "How can I help?" Manage our own helplessness and fear without imposing it on them. And . . . never, ever offer advice without asking permission. (This rule applies for adolescents also.)

My friend's daughter began using drugs in high school. Then she became quite promiscuous. She began to fail in school. By the time she was twenty-two years old, she had been in and out of rehab and was living in a home with unsavory characters in an unsafe neighborhood. My friend tried intervention—daily phone calls, a career counselor, and yet another rehab program. Everything failed. Finally her daughter told her mother not to call anymore. When she wanted contact, she would call.

My friend was filled with anguish. Her daughter was living in harm's way, and there was nothing my friend could do about it. But even when the stakes are life and death, the rules are the same. My friend now has to love her daughter from a distance, find a way to manage her helplessness, and respect her daughter's control over her own life.

Difficult? Hell, yes. I know.

What I've Learned About Wanting

❦

It's not unusual for me to be in the house by myself for long periods of time. I have pretty good access to every part of the house, and I can take care of my essential needs. But when things go wrong, there's no one to help me.

On this particular day, I was a little hungry and I knew I had a bag of pretzels in the snack drawer, so I navigated my way into the kitchen. The drawer is about eighteen inches below my wheelchair. I had to lean over to open the drawer. By tilting to one side and using the heel of my hand, I could grip the plastic bag and slide it up the side of my leg. Just as I was about to get the bag onto my lap, it fell, spraying pretzels across the floor.

What to do? The longer I looked at the pretzels, the hungrier I became. My nurse wouldn't be arriving for several hours. Meanwhile I had absolutely no way to recover the bag from the floor.

First my hunger became ravenous and it felt like I couldn't make it through another two hours without eating. Then I felt furious at this injustice and humiliation . . . which gave way to self-pity. And then I got it: What I felt just then was stronger than any real hunger. It was the emotion of desire. And as I sat there in the kitchen, looking at the pretzels on the floor, I could "watch" that emotion as it danced between my stomach and my mind.

About ten years ago, I reread *Siddhartha*, by Herman Hesse, a book that I had first read as a young man.

Hesse's interpretation of the awakening of the Buddha goes something like this. The Buddha was born a highly pampered and protected prince. One day he wandered outside the castle and in the process discovered the depths of human suffering. He was so intensely affected by what he experienced that he decided to devote his life to understanding this suffering and finding a way to alleviate it.

To become enlightened, the Buddha lived with various groups of people who were reputed to have wisdom. Among them were the ascetics, people who believed that enlightenment came from deprivation. In pursuit of that sought-after enlightenment, they deprived themselves of food, sleep, and other things that most of us feel are essential.

The first time I read *Siddhartha*, I had been left wondering what the value of this self-imposed suffering was. Even when I'd read it again, years later, I still didn't quite understand. But that day in the kitchen it all became clear. The purpose of deprivation was to learn how to tolerate desire.

What do I mean by this?

Every day in my office, I see people who desire something that they don't have. (I guess if they didn't *want*, they wouldn't have called me in the first place.) I hear many people talk about their desire to be different than they are. I hear husbands desiring more sex, and wives desiring more care. I hear a young adult woman tell me how much she wants her mother to assert herself with her controlling father. In another session, I hear from a dad who wants his son to try harder and perform better. And anybody who has suffered a trauma or a loss will tell me that what they want is what they had yesterday.

After my accident, all I wanted was to walk. Didn't happen. Then all I wanted was to have sensation. No. After that, all I wanted was to be able to move my fingers. That, too, was not in the cards. I reduced the size of my requests to the point where all I wanted was to be able to pee on my own. And you know what? That didn't happen either.

I guess I figured if my demands got smaller I would have a better chance of getting one of them. But, no, I didn't get any of the things I wanted.

So I understand when the wife of an active alcoholic tells me, "I'm not even asking him to stop drinking. All I want is for him *not to crash the car*. That's all! I think that's reasonable."

Of course it's reasonable. It's a very small request. But as long as her husband is drinking and as long as he has access to a car, her reasonable desire will probably never be realized.

So I often ask people what they want. The list is sometimes quite long. Then I ask them to imagine life without getting *any* of the things on the list. Of course, that is every person's worst nightmare. Many become angry just hearing the question.

Sometimes when they have finished listing all the things that come immediately to mind, I ask them what they *really* want.

Try to imagine what it would be like if the urgency of your desires simply went away. What if your life were just about as it is now, but your desires turned to simple wishes? No longer a loud demand for something that feels urgent, just a quiet wish for something not there.

Personally, what I want is *not to want*. In the time I have left, I want to be where I am, whether it is good or bad. I know I'll never get there, but that's what I want.

My experience with the pretzels taught me something. When we have loosened our grasp a bit for what we desire, the wanting turns into a longing, and then into a dull ache. I no longer need to walk or dance, but every now and then I can feel that dull ache. I don't know if this is true for all humans, but I have found that serenity increases as I learn to live comfortably with my longing.

Maybe that's what the Buddha learned. Desire is just a symptom of distress and not a call to action.

PEACE COMES ONLY WHEN WE STOP FIGHTING

My bacteria and my mind are in hot pursuit.

As far as the bacteria go, my urologist is the one keeping his eye on them. Because of all the antibiotics I've taken over the years to combat urinary tract infections, my urologist says the bacteria are "getting smarter." That's a big evolutionary step for the bacteria. To consider that the bacteria in my body are actually smarter then my bladder and more clever than most medications is really fascinating. But it gets less interesting (and pretty quickly) if you are the human with the bladder.

These smart bacteria remind me of a discovery I made many years ago when I first started studying Buddhism. When I began learning meditation, I discovered for the first time what it was like to look at my mind from the outside instead of living *inside* my mind and assuming that everything I thought and felt was accurate. As I applied this knowledge to my clinical work, I watched my patients as they frequently got lost inside their minds, listening to their critical voices as if they were the voices of truth rather than simply thoughts.

So many people I know feel an uncomfortable emotion like anxiety or insecurity or loneliness, and then work very hard to abate those emotions. They try to figure out the causes and blame the person or situation that caused the discomfort. They grasp at whatever they can in an effort to make those painful feelings go away.

As I watch my fellow humans and watch my own mind, I realize that our minds are much smarter then we are. When our inner critic tells us we are not good enough, we try harder to make the critic stop. It never works. When we listen to what our critic says, we still suffer. When we try to outsmart the critic or drug it, it still returns. No matter what we do, we will never outsmart our own minds.

Suppose you live with the demon of insecurity (as most of us do), and your reactive mind immediately pursues security to make that bad feeling go away. But it can't be done. No matter how hard we try, the demon outsmarts us—the message about *in*security keeps springing to mind, refusing to let us rest.

Even in the Bible it is said, "You shall take all the sins of the people and imbue the head of a goat with all of those sins and then banish the goat forever." Thus the origin of the term "scapegoat." Let's take all demons, give them to a goat, and ship them off. But that didn't work either. The goat keeps returning. (Notice the devil looks a lot like that goat, with horns and cloven hooves.) We just can't get away from our demons.

So here I am. I have a mind that is smarter than I am, well stocked with horrible demons that can wake me in the middle of the night and remind me of all of the potential problems I could face in life. And now I have bacteria that are smarter than my doctors. Sometimes I feel great anxiety about what is happening to me, as I sometimes feel my life winding down. When that happens, my instinct is to answer some of my e-mails or return phone calls or watch a movie or . . .

But when I can *sit* with the fear and not try to push it away, I feel great sadness—as I am reminded that my life, like everything precious, is temporary. Somehow, that sadness feels more real and truer than the anxiety. That's because, as uncomfortable as it is, the anxiety helps me avoid feeling what I really feel. But when I feel that sadness, I feel more alive, loving, and compassionate. At those times, I can truly experience my life and not categorize it as good or bad, easy or difficult. When I can just experience my life in all its fragility, everything seems more vivid. I feel my pleasure when I am with someone. When I look from my window or go out in the yard, I experience the clarity of the colors in the trees, the grass, the leaves, and the sky. I can feel openhearted love for most people, life itself, and every breath. I even have gratitude and compassion for my own bladder because it has worked so hard for so many years. When I feel these emotions, I truly experience life in its fullness, moment by moment.

Sometimes when I wonder how much time I have left, I think about one of the fellow students I met while taking a meditation course, a woman who was terminally ill. Learning meditation is a long process that can take years of dedication. So one day I asked her, Why begin at all when she might not have all those years?

She said, "All my life, wherever I was, I was always somewhere else. In the time I have left, I want to be where I am."

Me too.

THE 11ᵀᴴ COMMANDMENT

In *The History of World*, a Mel Brooks film, the director gets to cast himself in the part of Moses. Coming down from Mount Sinai after meeting God, Mel/Moses is carrying three tablets. Raising the tablets before the assembled Israelites, he proclaims, "God has given us *fifteen* . . ." at which point he stumbles and drops one of the tablets ". . . no, make that ten. God has given us *Ten* Commandments!"

Ever since seeing that movie, I've wondered what might have been on the other tablet. My theory is this: Commandment Eleven was, "Thou shalt not take thyself too seriously!"

We need such a commandment because I have noticed that all humans take themselves too seriously. We believe that our problems are more important than anyone else's. We believe that if we are hungry for something in our lives, that hunger is more important than all others.

It is written that the Buddha is recorded as having said, "If you could summarize all my teachings into just one, it would be this—to disavow everything beginning with 'I,' 'me,' or 'mine.'" Of course, none of us are very good at this. We tend to take ourselves *very* seriously.

Let's look at this: "me."

This is my book. These are my ideas. Only . . . not true! These aren't *my* ideas! They are ideas that have washed through me at some stage, and some have stayed with me. Why did they stay? Because of my learning disability? Because of my life experience? Because of love I received and love I lost? The way my mind works is not my doing—it's the blessing of having a mind that sees the world the way it does. Of course, that very same mind embodies more than its share of neuroses.

So here I am with these ideas that don't come *from* me but *through* me. And if they have an impact at any level on anyone, then you and I are both the recipients of some sort of blessing that has allowed us to touch one another. I am not a teacher; you are not a student. In this moment, if what has come through me has been a benefit to you, that doesn't make me smart. It makes us blessed with a connection that is the sum of everything that has passed through your mind and everything that passes through mine.

The truth is, we should live with the knowledge that we're not important at all as individuals. And—and I do mean *and*—everything we say and do counts. There is no personal pronoun in who-we-are. What matters is what we do.

Some time ago, I was giving a talk to a community group meeting in a Presbyterian Church. Suddenly the microphone went dead. The minister came on stage to get it working again. As we were kidding around, he said, "Oh, God would not let this happen. Not here—not now!"

"Well, maybe *your* God wouldn't," I replied.

Since the audience caught the remark and began to chuckle, I took this as permission to run with my thinking. When the sound system came up again, I continued, "Look, just the other day I was asking my God to help me out with something, and He said, 'Gottlieb leave me alone! I gave you the tools you need to work out your own problems! Me, I'm busy! It's autumn. I've got to get the leaves the right color, and I've got to get them down on time. Don't bother me!' "

The audience laughed, and so did I. But when I began to think more seriously about what I had just said, I realized this: In the broad scheme of things, my problems aren't all that important. And maybe I would be much happier if I paid closer attention to the divine work going on around me, rather than what I was worrying about. So now I'm thinking if Mel Brooks were to have written the final Five Commandments, life would be a lot more fun—and funny.

LIFE: THE GOOD NEWS AND THE BAD NEWS

So here we are with life, and it turns out to be a shaggy dog story. It's like the joke that that begins with, "I have good news and bad news."

When we are born, the good news is that, despite tremendous odds, we will have a life. The bad news is that we will likely be raised by parents who don't know what they are doing but pretend they do.

Good news? Many of us will find love and security in the home where we grow up. Bad news? Nearly half of us will live through a parental divorce and spend time living apart from a father. (Many others will go through that twice.)

And so it goes through life. Everything carries with it good news and bad news—adolescence, sexuality, marriage, child-rearing, and aging. Even trauma like my accident carries good news and bad news. I suffer, still get frustrated and sometimes depressed, and yet there is good news about being a quadriplegic.

The good news about being quadriplegic?

Well, first, there is the obvious—great parking spaces.

Then, think shoes. I don't have to spend a fortune on comfortable shoes, and they last as long as I want them to.

But the great news about quadriplegia is that I don't have to get up to pee in the middle of the night. So, in the middle of the night tonight, when you are sitting or standing, I'll be sleeping. (And they say *I* have special needs!)

On a more serious note, this disability has helped me become the man I am. The image I have carried for nearly thirty years is that when my neck broke, my soul began to breathe. Because of my differentness, I have not been intimidated by my need to be like everyone else. I might not have become the man I am today were it not for this trauma.

Several years ago, a young man and his mother came to see me for consultation. He was a strikingly handsome seventeen-year-old who had been a quadriplegic for three months. As you would expect, he looked frightened, confused, and depressed, and so did his mother.

I do this kind of thing often, so I pretty much knew they were looking for guidance. They needed a sense that the future had some possibilities.

The consultation went well. The three of us spoke for a while about their concerns, their fears, and mechanical issues (changing catheters, managing one's bowels, wheel-chair repairs, etc.). Then the young man and I spoke privately. He and his girlfriend had broken up shortly after the accident, and he wondered how sexuality worked. I told him that we can make love with our eyes, our voices, our fingers, and our mouths. Sex would not be as good as it had been before, I said, but it was still wonderful. I told him that sometimes I felt myself having close to an orgasm when I held my partner close as she had one.

After the young man and I had talked alone, his mother returned and I took them for a tour around my house. I showed them how the bathroom and bedroom worked, where my nurses stayed—in a way that gave me a boundary—and how I made meals. Then I showed them the van that I drive independently. The young man's eyes lit up.

At the end of the session, mother and son both looked much better than they had at the beginning. As they thanked me, they were smiling. They saw hope that their future lives had the potential for happiness. And I smiled, satisfied that they received what they needed.

Then, when they left my office and the door closed, I began to cry. I cried for all of the suffering this beautiful young man would endure. I cried for the years of frustration and loneliness he would feel. I cried for all of the hungers he would feel that could never be satisfied. I cried for him, I cried for me, and I cried for all of us.

Was I lying when I didn't tell him these feelings? I don't think so. I wasn't even conscious of those feelings when the young man and his mother were with me. And everything I did tell them was true. My life is good and precious. I love almost everything about it. I feel more gratitude and awe and love then most humans I know. My life is a blessing.

And yet I suffer. And I sometimes feel despair.

⌒⨯⌒

Even death carries good news and bad news, and I've treated many people who have lost a parent with whom they've had a complicated relationship.

I recently worked with a man whose father was alcoholic and tyrannical and sometimes violent with the family. As he aged, my patient tried to make amends with his father, with only partial success. The son held the fear and resentment in his bones. And then when his father died, he felt relief. But he also lost hope of ever connecting with the father he always longed to have.

When my mother died, my father suffered terribly. He couldn't sleep, felt great guilt, and thought about her all day. And then he noticed, after a while, that his suffering was diminished and there were times when he *wasn't* thinking about her. And he felt guilt about not suffering. Life, death, good news, bad news.

As I age and my urinary tract begins to fatigue, I feel I am living the last chapter of my life (hoping it will be a pretty long one). So when I think about my death, of course I find good news and bad news. The bad news? I will never be able to embrace my children and grandson again. I will never be able to love all of the people and things that make my life so rich. The good news? No more wheelchairs, catheters, medications, and on and on. I'll never have to watch people dance and pretend I don't mind that I can't.

There is a yoga saying: "To experience is to live. To explain is to lie."

When I can fully experience my life, I can feel my suffering and deprivation, and I can experience the slow, steady deterioration of my body. And I can also feel the treasures of life I experience every day. During those times when I can feel death kissing me on one cheek and life kissing me on the other, I am fully awake, fully alive, feeling despair, futility, suffering, love, gratitude, and awe.

And I know that what is going on in my brain, my body, and my soul is exactly what's going on with other humans. Maybe the only difference is that I can feel all of these things. And that's good news and bad news.

But despite death bringing good news and bad news, I have instructed one of my friends to say the following at my funeral: "Out of everyone in this room, Dan is pretty pissed that he has to be the one in the box!"

FINAL THOUGHTS

I recently had a conversation in my office with a thirteen-year-old girl I'll call Charlotte. Charlotte's blue eyes, big heart, and warm smile don't tell the story of her painful history of loss and neglect.

As our meetings often do, this one began with her observations about my office as she wondered about all of the extra books and papers on my desk. When I told her I was writing a book, she became very curious and asked what it was about. As soon as I told her it was about what it means to be human, I thought she might have some special insight because, in her short lifetime, she had seen the best and worst of humanity.

Charlotte's mother died when Charlotte was three years old. Her father was not equipped to care for Charlotte and her sister, so a family member took custody.

Charlotte's hard times didn't end with her mother's death. The intense mourning and fear of a very young child was difficult, and when she started school, she had trouble adjusting. It was a challenge for her to trust that parent figures wouldn't abandon her. So this child with a sweet, generous heart and a wounded soul had to figure out how to navigate this thing called life on her own.

I first met her several years ago, and, since then, I have provided her with consistent and predictable care and she has provided me with great insights into a child's ability to be resilient in the face of tragedy. So when I described to Charlotte what this book was about, I thought perhaps she might have some insights that would help me summarize a subject that probably could not be summarized.

"So, Charlotte, what do you think it means to be human?" I asked.

"I don't know, it could mean anything."

I could tell from her response that the question was too big and too abstract, so she fumbled with it. I tried again.

"Okay, then, so what is it like to be you?"

"Sometimes it's pretty hard. Wherever I go, I am the only one without a mother and who doesn't live with either of their parents."

"So what's that like?"

"Well, when I feel that way, I feel really alone and different from the other kids. I feel a little scared and sad. I feel like nobody understands me. And sometimes I don't like myself. That's because when I get real scared, sometimes I get angry. And then when I calm down, I hate what I did."

"So you feel scared and insecure sometimes. And sometimes your emotions get so big that you will do almost anything to make them calm down," I summarized.

"Yes," she agreed. "And sometimes I'm not even thinking about those things and I am just happy. I am happy when I am watching *American Idol* with my aunt, or happy when I do well in school, or when I go to the Phillies game with my uncle. Actually, I am happy a lot of time." There was a moment's pause. "And when I think of my mother, I feel so sad."

"So, sometimes you feel very lonely and misunderstood," I repeated. "Sometimes you feel scared and abandoned. And sometimes you get scared of your own emotions. Sometimes you hate yourself because you are not as good as you think you should be, and sometimes you just enjoy your life and love the people who love you."

My grandson Sam has autism, and he's about six years younger than Charlotte, so I can't have the same kind of talk with Sam that I've had with Charlotte. But because of Sam's autism, his brain works a little differently from most, and he has unique insights into what it means to be human.

When Sam gets overstimulated, he has "meltdowns." As a toddler, he would bang his head on the floor. With therapy, these episodes have become less dangerous and more predictable. On a recent visit, Sam had one of his meltdowns. I watched his breathing get rapid and his face red. Then his body became rigid and he raged about himself and everyone else, insisting he be left alone before collapsing on the floor sobbing. A few minutes later, after allowing my daughter to hold him on her lap as he cried, Sam looked up and said, "Mommy, everything just went too fast inside my head today."

This is something most of us could say. We don't, because we don't feel the pain that Sam feels. But it's in there, just like the anxiety of the people who visited my bedside. They didn't feel the anxiety, but it was in there.

So we go through our lives at lightning speed and don't feel the pain our mind/body feels. But Sam does.

And we go through our lives dealing with our abandonment, insecurity, and self-judgment and don't feel the vulnerability that goes with those emotions. But Charlotte does.

And we go through our lives knowing in our hearts that one day we will die, and that day will be here sooner than we would like it to be. But our brains don't quite believe that. Our hearts know how precious life is, but most of us don't feel that. I do.

So what does it mean to be human? You must decide on your own, but here is what I recommend:

When you see a fellow human, first notice the indentation on the other person's top lip (God's fingerprint, same as yours).

Then look in the other person's eyes. You will find a human who is tender and vulnerable, one who pursues security, happiness, and love. You will find someone who is capable of great, selfless compassion and one who can be terribly self-centered. You will find someone who has been hurt and who, in turn, has hurt others. You will see a hypocrite, a child, an orphan, a warrior, and a hero. You will see someone who wants more love. And if you look deeply into another person's eyes, you will see that person's soul. And then you will discover what you have always known about your own humanity.

AFTERWORD

I've had several people tell me after funerals that they wished the deceased had heard the beautiful eulogies while they were still living. As a result, I've been encouraging people to say goodbye to the people they care about as though they will not have that chance again. Tell them what they mean to you, how they make you feel, and what you would wish for them if you never saw them again.

Given my philosophy, my age, and my health, I have written this book as though it will be my last. I have told you stories and beliefs as though my stories will end with this book. At times, my neurotic mind interfered greatly with the process: Did I say it the right way? Did I mention this or that story? If this is my last chance, is my message clear? This is just my mind trying to grasp a legacy, hoping that goodbye really isn't goodbye.

I have told many people that my body is broken, my mind is neurotic, and my soul is at peace. Much as I try to avoid it, sometimes I live inside my mind. At this moment, I live inside my soul. From that place, I feel great gratitude and humility. I'm deeply grateful that you have read my words. I'm humbled that little Danny Gottlieb from Atlantic City would be invited to open his heart and mind and share it with you. I thank you for your trust, your time, and your connection.

At this moment, our last moment, I feel tenderhearted. I feel love.

I wish the same for you.

Love After Love

by Derek Walcott

The time will come
when, with elation,
you will greet yourself arriving
at your own door, in your own mirror,
and each will smile at the other's welcome,

and say, sit here. Eat.
You will love again the stranger who was your self.
Give wine. Give bread. Give back your heart
to itself, to the stranger who has loved you

all your life, whom you ignored
for another, who knows you by heart.
Take down the love letters from the bookshelf,

the photographs, the desperate notes,
peel your own image from the mirror.
Sit. Feast on your life.